BASIC LABORATORY EXERCISES FOR FORENSIC SCIENCE

RICHARD SAFERSTEIN, Ph.D.

PEARSON

Prentice Hall

Upper Saddle River, New Jersey 07458

Editor-in-Chief: Vernon R., Anthony
Executive Editor: Frank Mortimer, Jr.
Assistant Editor: Mayda Bosco
Marketing Manager: Adam Kloza
Editorial Assistant: Jillian Allison
Production Editor: Lindsey Hancock, Carlisle Editorial Services
Production Liaison: Barbara Marttine Cappuccio
Director of Manufacturing and Production: Bruce Johnson
Managing Editor: Mary Carnis
Manufacturing Manager: Ilene Sanford
Manufacturing Buyer: Cathleen Petersen
Cover Designer: Denise Brown
Cover Images: Microscope, Check Carlton, Index Stock Imagery, Inc.; Thumbprint, Andy Caufield, Getty Images, Inc.; Shoe print, Andy Crawford, Dorling Kindersley Media Library
Printing and Binding: Bind-Rite Graphics

Pearson Education Ltd.
Pearson Education Singapore, Pte. Ltd.
Pearson Education Canada, Ltd.
Pearson Education—Japan
Pearson Education Australia PTY, Limited
Pearson Education North Asia Ltd.
Pearson Educación de Mexico, S.A. de C.V.
Pearson Education Malaysia, Pte. Ltd.

10 9 8 7 6 5 4 3
ISBN: 0-13-221627-2
(high school edition) ISBN: 0-13-196143-8

Sarah A. Skorupsky-Borg, MSFS invested an extraordinary amount of time and effort in assisting in the preparation of this laboratory manual. Her skills and tenacity in carrying out this task are acknowledged and greatly appreciated.

Contents

Safety Symbols

These symbols alert you to possible dangers.

Safety Goggles Always wear safety goggles to protect your eyes in any activity involving chemicals, flames, or heating, or the possibility of broken glassware.

Laboratory Apron Wear a laboratory apron to protect your skin and clothing.

Breakage You are working with breakable materials, such as glassware. Handle breakable materials with care. Do not touch broken glassware.

Heat-Resistant Gloves Use hand protection when handling hot materials. Hot equipment or hot water can cause burns. Do not touch hot objects with your bare hands.

Plastic Gloves Wear disposable plastic gloves to protect yourself from chemicals or organisms that could be harmful. Keep your hands away from your face. Dispose of the gloves according to your teacher's instructions at the end of the activity.

Heating Use a clamp or tongs to pick up hot glassware. Do not touch hot objects with your bare hands.

Sharp Object Pointed-tip scissors, scalpels, knives, needles, pins, or tacks can cut or puncture your skin. Always direct a sharp edge or point away from yourself and others. Use sharp instruments only as directed.

Electric Shock Avoid the possibility of electric shock. Never use electrical equipment around water, or when equipment is wet or your hands are wet. Be sure cords are untangled and cannot trip anyone. Disconnect the equipment when it is not in use.

Corrosive Chemical Avoid getting acids or other corrosive chemicals on your skin or clothing, or in your eyes. Do not inhale the vapors. Wash your hands when you are finished with the activity.

Poison Do not let any poisonous chemical come in contact with your skin, and do not inhale its vapors. Wash your hands when you are finished with the activity.

Physical Safety When an experiment involves physical activity, take precautions to avoid injuring yourself or others. Follow instructions from your teacher. Alert your teacher if there is any reason you should not participate in the activity.

Animal Safety Treat live animals with care to avoid harming the animals or yourself. Working with animal parts or preserved animals also may require caution. Wash your hands when you are finished.

Plant Safety Handle plants only as directed by your teacher. If you are allergic to certain plants, tell your teacher before doing an activity in which plants are used. Avoid touching poisonous plants or plants with thorns. Wash your hands when you are finished with the activity.

Flames You may be working with flames from a Bunsen burner, candle, or matches. Tie back loose hair and clothing. Follow instructions from your teacher about lighting and extinguishing flames.

No Flames Flammable materials may be present. Make sure no flames, sparks, or exposed heat sources are present.

Fumes When poisonous or unpleasant vapors may be involved, work in a ventilated area. Avoid inhaling vapors directly. Only test an odor when directed to do so by your teacher, and use a wafting motion to direct the vapor toward your nose.

Disposal Chemicals and other used materials must be disposed of safely. Follow the instructions from your teacher.

Hand Washing Wash your hands thoroughly. Use antibacterial soap and warm water. Lather both sides of your hands and between your fingers. Rinse well.

General Safety Awareness You may see this symbol when none of the other symbols appears. In this case, follow the specific instructions provided. You may also see this symbol when you are asked to develop your own procedure. Have your teacher approve your plan before you go further.

Science Safety Rules

One of the first things a scientist learns is that working in the laboratory can be an exciting experience. But the laboratory can also be quite dangerous if proper safety rules are not followed at all times. To prepare yourself for a safe year in the laboratory, read over the following safety rules. Then read them a second time. Make sure you understand each rule. If you do not, ask your teacher to explain any rules you are unsure of.

Dress Code

1. Many materials in the laboratory can cause eye injury. To protect yourself from possible injury, wear safety goggles whenever you are working with chemicals, burners, or any substance that might get into your eyes. Never wear contact lenses in the laboratory.

2. Wear a laboratory apron or coat whenever you are working with chemicals or heated substances.

3. Tie back long hair to keep your hair away from any chemicals, burners and candles, or other laboratory equipment.

4. Remove or tie back any article of clothing or jewelry that can hang down and touch chemicals and flames. Do not wear sandals or open-toed shoes in the laboratory. Never walk around the laboratory barefoot or in stocking feet.

General Safety Rules

5. Be serious and alert when working in the laboratory. Never "horse around" in the laboratory.

6. Be prepared to work when you arrive in the laboratory. Be sure that you understand the procedure to be employed in any laboratory investigation and the possible hazards associated with it.

7. Read all directions for an investigation several times. Follow the directions exactly as they are written. If you are in doubt about any part of the investigation, ask your teacher for assistance.

8. Never perform activities that are not authorized by your teacher. Obtain permission before "experimenting" on you own.

9. Never handle any equipment unless you have specific permission.

10. Take extreme care not to spill any material in the laboratory. If spills occur, ask your teacher immediately about the proper cleanup procedure. Never simply pour chemicals or other substances into the sink or trash container.

11. Never eat or taste anything or apply cosmetics in the laboratory unless directed to do so. This includes food, drinks, candy, and

gum, as well as chemicals. Wash your hands before and after performing every investigation.

12. Know the location and proper use of safety equipment such as the fire extinguisher, emergency blanket, first-aid kit, emergency shower, and eyewash station.

13. Notify your teacher of any medical problems you may have, such as allergies or asthma.

14. Keep your laboratory area clean and free of unnecessary books, papers, and equipment.

First Aid

15. Report all accidents, no matter how minor, to your teacher immediately.

16. Learn what to do in case of specific accidents such as getting acid in your eyes or on your skin. (Rinse acid off your body with lots of water.)

17. Become aware of the location of the first-aid kit. Your teacher should administer any required first-aid due to injury. Or your teacher may send you to the school nurse or call a physician.

18. Know where and how to report an accident or fire. Find out the location of the fire extinguisher, phone, and fire alarm. Keep a list of important phone numbers such as the fire department and school nurse near the phone. Report any fires to your teacher at once.

Heating and Fire Safety

19. Never use a heat source such as a candle or burner without wearing safety goggles.

20. Never heat a chemical you are not instructed to heat. A chemical that is harmless when cool can be dangerous when heated.

21. Maintain a clean work area and keep all materials away from flames.

22. Never reach across a flame.

23. Make sure you know how to light a Bunsen burner. (Your teacher will demonstrate the proper procedure for lighting a burner.) If the flame leaps out of a burner toward you, turn the gas off immediately. Do not touch the burner. It may be hot. And never leave a lighted burner unattended.

24. Point a test tube or bottle that is being heated away from you and others. Chemicals can splash or boil out of a heated test tube.

25. Never heat a liquid in a closed container. The expanding gases produced may blow the container apart, injuring you or others.

26. Never pick up a container that has been heated without first holding the back of your hand near it. If you can feel the heat on the back of your hand, the container may be too hot to handle. Use a clamp, tongs, or heat-resistant gloves when handling hot containers.

Using Chemicals Safely

27. Never mix chemicals for the "fun of it." You might produce a dangerous, possibly explosive, substance.

28. Never touch, taste, or smell a chemical that you do not know for a fact is harmless. Many

chemicals are poisonous. If you are instructed to note the fumes in an investigation, gently wave your hand over the opening of a container and direct the fumes toward your nose. Do not inhale the fumes directly form the container.

29. Use only those chemicals needed in the investigation. Keep all lids closed when a chemical is not being used. Notify your teacher whenever chemicals are spilled.

30. Dispose of all chemicals as instructed by your teacher. To avoid contamination, never return chemicals to their original containers.

31. Be extra careful when working with acids or bases. Pour such chemicals over the sink, not over your workbench.

32. When diluting an acid, pour the acid into water. Never pour water into the acid.

33. Rinse any acids off your skin or clothing with water. Immediately notify your teacher of any acid spill.

Using Glassware Safely

34. Never force glass tubing into a rubber stopper. A turning motion and lubricant will be helpful when inserting glass tubing into rubber stoppers or rubber tubing. Your teacher will demonstrate the proper way to insert glass tubing.

35. Never heat glassware that is not thoroughly dry. Use a wire screen to protect glassware from any flame.

36. Keep in mind that hot glassware will not appear hot. Never pick up glassware without first checking to see if it is hot.

37. If you are instructed to cut glass tubing, fire polish the ends immediately to remove sharp edges.

38. Never use broken or chipped glassware. If glassware breaks, notify your teacher and dispose of the glassware in the proper trash container.

39. Never eat or drink from laboratory glassware. Clean glassware thoroughly before putting it away.

Using Sharp Instruments

40. Handle scalpels or razor blades with extreme care. Never cut material toward you; cut away from you.

41. Be careful when handling sharp, pointed objects such as scissors, pins, and dissecting probes.

42. Notify your teacher immediately if you cut yourself or receive a cut.

Handling Living Organisms

43. No investigations that will cause pain, discomfort, or harm to mammals, birds, reptiles, fish, and amphibians should be done in the classroom or at home.

44. Treat all living things with care and respect. Do not touch any organism in the classroom or laboratory unless given permission to do so. Many plants are poisonous or have thorns, and even tame animals may bite or scratch if alarmed.

45. Animals should be handled only if necessary. If an animal is excited or frightened, pregnant, feeding, or with its young, special handling is required.

46. Your teacher will instruct you as to how to handle each species that may be brought into the classroom.

47. Treat all microorganisms as if they were harmful. Use antiseptic procedure, as directed by your teacher, when working with microbes. Dispose of microbes as your teacher directs.

48. Clean your hands thoroughly after handling animals or the cage containing animals.

49. Wear gloves when handling small mammals. Report animal bites or stings to your teacher at once.

End-of-Investigation Rules

50. When an investigation is completed, clean up your work area and return all equipment to its proper place.

51. Wash your hands with soap and warm water after every investigation.

52. Turn off all burners before leaving the laboratory. Check that the gas line leading to the burner is off as well.

List of Materials and Equipment

Item	Quantity, per group	Exercise #
0.75-inch weather stripping nails	5	6
A-B-O/Rh Simulated blood kit	1	12
Agar	1 gram	12
Aluminum bars of varying length	several	4
Aluminum foil, 5″ square	1	16
Balance	1	4
Beaker, 250-mL	1	12, 13
Blotter paper	1 foot square	11
Blue ball-point pens	5	8, 9, 10
Butcher paper or bench drape	~	1
Calcium chloride, 2M solution	approx. 1 mL	12
Camera, digital	1	3
Camera, digital or film	1	11
Capillary tubes	10	9, 10, 13
Cardboard (or manilla)	1 foot square	11
Cardboard box, at least 12 inches square	1	4
Chromatography paper	several squares	9
Coffee can, 3-lb. size	1	16
Coplin jar	1	9, 10, 13
Cotton balls	2	7
Cotton swab, wooden, single ended	12	12
Coverslips	1 box	6, 7
Craft stick	1	14, 15
Desk lamp	1	8
Envelopes	several	1
Ethanol, 95 percent, with dropper bottle	approx. 10 mL	10, 13
Ethyl acetate	approx. 15 mL	10, 13
Fingerprint powder application brush, fiberglass	2	5
Fingerprint powder, black	approx. 1 Tbsp	5
Fingerprint powder, white	approx. 1 Tbsp	5
Foil fuming trays, disposable	3	5
Forceps	1	1, 6, 7
Glass microscope slides	1 box	1, 5, 6, 7, 13
Glass pane	1	4
Glass samples (broken)	~	4

Glass specimen jars with lids, 4-oz.	several	16
Glycerin or propylene glycol solution	several drops	7
Graduated cylinder, 10-mL	1	13
Graduated cylinder, 100-mL	1	4
Graduated cylinder, 10-mL	1	10
Hair samples, human	at least 3	7
Hair samples, nonhuman	at least 3	7
Hair spray, aerosol	1 can per class	15
Hammer	1	4
Hand lens	1	1, 4, 6, 7, 14, 15, 16
Hand tools (vise grips, pliers, screwdriver, etc.)	4 to 6	14
Hemastix®	several	12
Hotplate or microwave oven	1	12, 13
Hydrogen peroxide (3%) solution, in a dropper bottle	1	12
Index card	1	5
Iodine crystals	approx. 1 Tbsp	5, 13
Isopropyl aclohol (rubbing alcohol)	approx. 250 mL	7, 16
Latex balloons, white	3	5
Liquid lip color samples	at least 3 brands	13
Liver, beef or chicken	0.5 lb	12, 16
Marker, permanent	1	4, 16
Matchbooks	several	6
Measuring tape, at least 72″ long	1	11, 17
Methanol, 100 percent	2 mL	9
Microscope, compound	1	6
Microscope, stereoscopic	1	1, 6, 7, 14
Mixing bowl and spoon	1 set	15
Modeling clay	1/4 of a small package	6, 14
Mug warmer	1	5, 13
Nail polish, clear	1 bottle	7
Newspaper clipping	a 2-inch square	6
Oregano or catnip, dried	1/8 tsp	6
Paper punch, 1-hole	1	16
Paper roll, white, at least 36″ wide	one-6-foot length	11
Paper, unlined	1 per student	5, 8
Pencil with eraser	1	3, 5, 9, 10, 13
Petri dish	2	12
Phenolphthalein solution, in a dropper bottle	several drops	12
Pipe cleaners, various colors and lengths	several	16
Pipette (Pasteur) with bulb	3	9, 11, 13
Pipette (plastic)	10	11

Plaster of Paris	5 lb	15
Plastic soda straw	1	12
Potassium phosphate tribasic, 1M solution	approx. 1 mL	12
Protractor	1	11
Reagent storage bottle, 100-mL	1	10
Ruler	1	3, 7, 9, 10, 13, 14, 15, 16, 17
Scissors or razor blade	1	6, 9
Shoebox	1	15
Silicone caulk	2-3 Tbsp	14
Simulated blood (purchased or homemade)	approx. 1 cup	11
SIRCHIE Insta-FumeTent™	1	5
Sketch book (grid-ruled paper)	1 per student	3
Soda can, emptied	1	5
Sodium polytungstate solution	approx. 5 mL	4
Soil or sand	at least 1 quart	15
Spot plate, 12-wells	1	9, 10
Storage bottle, 100 mL	2	9, 13
Styrofoam block	6×2 inch	12
Superglue®	1 tube	5
Thermometer, outdoor	1	16
Thermoplastic ink pad	1	5
Timer	1	16
Tissue culture dish, 60 mm disposable	1	5
TLC plates (precoated)	4	10, 13
Tooling foil, aluminum or copper	5″ × 5″ sheet	14
Toothpicks, plain wood	6	9, 12
Transparent tape (gift-wrapping type)	6-inch strip	5
T-shirt, white	1	1
Vermiculite	approx. 1 cup	16
Watchglass, 3-inch	1	5, 13
Water, distilled or deionized	approx. 10 mL	10, 13
Water, from tap	as needed	4, 15
Water, in a dropper bottle	1	5, 6
Water, sterile, in a dropper bottle	1	12
Wire hanger	2	15
Wood block	2	4, 14
Zip-top bag, 1-gallon size	2	1, 15
Zip-top bag, sandwich size	several	16

Locard's Exchange Principle in Action[1]

Edmond Locard (1877–1966) in 1910 persuaded the police department in Lyons, France, to give him two attic rooms and two assistants to start the world's first police laboratory.

During his first years of work, the only instruments available to Locard were a microscope and a rudimentary spectrometer. However, his enthusiasm quickly overcame the technical and monetary deficiencies he encountered. From these modest beginnings, Locard's research and accomplishments became known throughout the world by forensic scientists and criminal investigators.

It was Locard's belief that when a criminal came in contact with an object or person, a cross-transfer of evidence occurred (**Locard's Exchange Principle**). Locard strongly believed that every criminal can be connected to a crime by dust particles carried from the crime scene. This concept was reinforced by a series of successful and well-publicized investigations. In one case, confronted with counterfeit coins and the names of three suspects, Locard urged the police to bring the suspects' clothing to his laboratory. Upon careful examination, he located small metallic particles in all the garments. Chemical analysis revealed that the particles and coins were composed of exactly the same metallic elements. Confronted with this evidence, the suspects were arrested and soon confessed to the crime.

Every time you make contact with a person or object there is an exchange of materials. This could mean the transfer of fibers, hairs, wood shavings, metal filings, tidbits of paper, or any small, lightweight item adherent to the donor object. This exchange

---

[1] Courtesy Joanne Long, faculty of Cherry Hill East High School, Cherry Hill, New Jersey.

enables forensic scientists to determine where someone has been based on trace evidence. It is even possible to track a person's daily movements by examining his or her clothing.

MATERIALS

Forceps
Hand lens
Several small envelopes or sheets of notepaper
Microscope and slides

For this activity you will need **ONE** of the following:

- A new T-shirt, taken directly from the package, *or*
- A T-shirt that has been washed and dried separately. Otherwise, fabrics washed along with the T-shirt will transfer fibers. The lint screen of your tumble dryer must be well cleaned beforehand.

Day One

1. Wear your T-shirt on the day before the laboratory period.
2. Record your movements during the day. Describe the type of location and the people, animals, and activities you encounter. At the end of the day, seal the T-shirt in a zip-top bag and bring it into school.

Day Two

1. Clean the laboratory bench top with soap and water and then cover it with butcher paper, plastic sheeting, or a trash bag to inhibit contamination.
2. Lay the T-shirt flat on the bench top.
3. Using a hand lens and forceps, scan the shirt for any hairs or fibers and remove them using the forceps. Place the hairs and fibers you find inside small envelopes or use a clean sheet of paper to make druggist folds. Take special care around the collar area.
4. Turn the shirt over and repeat this process.
5. Examine your fibers under the microscope.
6. Group together hairs or fibers that look the same.
7. Try to identify each group based on your movements while wearing the shirt.

Crime Scene Investigation: A Case of Deductive Reasoning[2, 3]

INTRODUCTION

Insects are found in nearly every habitat on earth. Those who study insects are called **entomologists**. Forensic entomologists aid criminal investigations by applying their knowledge of insect activity to the circumstances of a case, usually a murder or suspicious death.

Many species rely on carrion, or dead animal carcasses, to serve as nurseries for their eggs and food for the hatched larvae. Once a larva has matured, it will secrete a substance around itself that soon hardens, called a pupa. Inside its new shell, the pupa will mature into its adult form, recognizable as those annoying outdoor pests. After mating, an adult female fly searches for a suitable carcass on which to lay her eggs, thus restarting the life cycle. In warm or hot weather, any number of species of flies will arrive to lay eggs almost immediately after an animal dies, guided by the smell of decaying flesh. Within the first hour after death, eggs are deposited in the orifices and/or wounds on a body, where larvae will find the easiest path under the skin. The hundreds of fly species have been studied so thoroughly that the timing of their life cycles is known to within hours or even minutes depending on temperature, time of day, and weather conditions. Based on these inevitable circuits, a forensic

---

[2] Contributed by Sarah A. Skorupsky-Borg, MSFS.

[3] Please refer to the *Instructor's Manual* for additional instructions relating to this experiment.

entomologist can determine the approximate time that a fly first arrived at a body.

Oviposition, or egg-laying, can be calculated to determine the approximate time of death—or, more properly, the **post-mortem interval (PMI)** since death. The PMI is the block of time that has elapsed between the moment of death and some point later, usually when the body was discovered. For investigative purposes, this kind of determination is considered as reliable as a medical examiner's opinion; and in some cases, a body that has been dead far too long for a medical doctor to be of help can be successfully examined by a forensic entomologist.

As a side note, another variable that can be resolved by an entomologist is the geographical area of a crime scene. Insects have a limited range due to temperature, elevation above sea level, and humidity requirements. If a body is discovered in a location uninhabited by the insects it carries, this is a clue the body has been moved to mislead investigators.

The samples collected are handled in two ways: some maggots are preserved in a protein fixative, and some are kept alive in a fly-rearing container. The preserved specimens are retained as evidence in the case. The live maggots are reared and allowed to pupate. Once the adult flies emerge, they are preserved and used to identify the fly species found on the body. This confirmation step supplies the necessary legal proof that belies the entomologist's findings.

When collecting insect specimens, the most important information to include is the date and location of collection. Without these data, the specimen is useless to an investigator. In total, each sample should be labeled with date, time and location, case identifier, specimen identification number, and the initials or signature of the collector. There will be eggs and larvae of varying ages, but the oldest of the cohort will provide the earliest possible time of oviposition. These are usually found in the head or face of the victim. In addition, these are the most essential specimens to determine how long the victim has been dead, which may differ significantly from how long the victim has been at the crime scene.

The black blow fly (*Phormia regina*) average life cycle is described in Exercise 16. This species is sensitive to temperature and will delay oviposition for 12 to 24 hours depending on the weather. It is important to note that blow flies will not deposit eggs during the nighttime hours or in the rain.

CASE STUDY

08:00 MONDAY MAY 14—POLICE RESPOND TO A REPORT OF A MISSING PERSON AT MIDDLE STATE UNIVERSITY

Professor Kline, director of the Anthropology Department at MSU, was reported missing by his assistant, Marcy. She appears inconsolable as she tensely straightens the already perfect alignment of her stapler, penholder, and desk blotter.

She explains, "He was due back this morning from a last-minute field trip. I'm sure everything's fine, but I can't help feeling like something's wrong!"

Now breaking into full-blown sobs, Marcy adds, "I got worried when he didn't come to work this morning or leave me a message. . . . I always ask him where he can be reached, but I didn't this time—he was in such a hurry to leave, I didn't want to bother him! Now, I . . . I . . . I can't tell you where he is!"

"I'm just so worried because Professor Kline always checks in when he changes his plans," squeaks Marcy. "Oh, I have a terrible feeling about this!"

You ask Officer Stransky, a bewildered but harmless-looking rookie, to take Marcy's statement. Thirty minutes and more than half a box of facial tissue later, he is able to relay her report. Mercifully, he has prepared an abridged version.

"According to Marcy, Professor Kline left for a field trip located near, uh, Jacob's Falls at around 5:15 last Friday night, or, uh, 17:15 hours. She indicates that's about 45 minutes from here. She said the Professor received a phone call from a Dr. Ralph Myers around 16:00 hours. He is an archaeologist and former student of, uh, Mr. Kline. Marcy says she answered the phone, as usual, and spoke to Dr. Myers briefly. Uh, she described Dr. Myers as sounding happy and upbeat, and anxious for the Professor to join him at what she called 'the site.' When I asked her what this means and what these two guys would be doing, she said she assumes, uh, Kline would assist Dr. Myers at an archie, archieo . . . uh, scientific dig. She said it is new and pretty important. It's somewhere along Cedar Creek, near Jacob's Falls. Apparently that's where this Dr. Myers guy is working. She also said that she called Dr. Myers' office at the community college twice this morning and got no answer. Oh, and if you can believe it, none of these guys owns a cell phone! I guess they're trying to live in the Stone Age, not just study it, right?!"

After thanking Stransky for his failed attempt at levity and what, as it turns out, was his inaugural witness statement, you decide to investigate Dr. Myers in a more official way. A Motor Vehicle Services check shows that Dr. Myers has a home on the coast, some 250 miles away. You don't like road trips, but it is definitely better than helping the Crime Scene Unit process Professor Kline's office. Anyway, Officer Stransky offers to drive. He has been tolerable thus far and he promises to not play country music. After some consideration you decide that's the best deal you're going to get all day.

08:30 TUESDAY MAY 15—ARRIVAL AT THE MYERS RESIDENCE

Dr. Myers' house is bright and clean, with handsome landscaping and a tire swing in the front yard. You and Stransky are greeted by his wife, Janine. She is covered in what appears to be finger paint, or maybe it's mustard, and there is the unmistakable sound of child-borne bedlam coming from the kitchen.

"Ma'am, is your husband Dr. Ralph Myers?" you ask.

"I never know where he is or when he's coming home," Mrs. Myers replies, defensively. "He lives out of a motel in Jacob's Falls. We see him when it's too rainy to dig or when he runs out of clean clothes."

"Actually, it's the *only* motel in Jacob's Falls, isn't it?" adds Stransky.

"He has an office in the community college, right Mrs. Myers? Would it be all right with you if we searched there?" you try to recover the conversation. Janine has drifted off, staring at her perfectly painted porch floor.

"Searched?. . . Yes, yes . . . sure," she says in a surprisingly weak voice. "You don't think. . . . The last time I spoke with him was on Friday night. He called from the hotel to tuck the kids into bed. We hung up around 9:00 p.m. I reported him missing Saturday night when he didn't call. He said he would call . . . around 8:30." Janine trails off, looking worried.

"Thanks for your help. We'll be in touch," you say, making a quick exit.

"Gosh, I though she was going to cry there, for a minute," says Stransky.

Knowingly you reply, "Yeah, she seems pretty shaken up." Days have passed and no one has heard from either Professor Kline or Dr. Myers.

10:05 TUESDAY MAY 15—SEARCH OF DR. MYERS' OFFICE

It's getting late, so you and Stransky double time it to the community college to check out Dr. Myers' office. You search his desk, bookcases, filing cabinets, and all the piles of papers and exams lying about—no luck. There is no indication of where he was digging, and if he kept a date book, it's not there.

"Let's get out of here, I'm starving! We missed breakfast and I'm starting to feel faint," says Stransky, rolling his eyes.

You consider how much effort it would be to drag him, swooning, out to the car. Just as you decide it would be best to leave him behind if he faints from hunger, a very young-looking student barges in.

"*What are you doing in here*?!" she barks.

Apparently Dr. Myers has a research assistant.

Emily Wilson, who looks way too young to be a graduate student, is unable to provide any new information concerning his whereabouts.

She explains, "Dr. Myers was a very secretive and competitive man. I could never get him to tell me exactly where the dig site is—and he's always been so jealous of Professor Kline I'm surprised he would even tell Kline about it. I don't know why Ralph talks to him at all. It's like he wishes he could be as famous as his great mentor. Anyway, you need a spectacular find to be famous in the field of archaeology. . . . I got the impression he finally had one at Jacob's Falls."

"Where were you last weekend?" you ask, noting the disdain in her voice as she said those last few words.

"I was at a young archaeologist's conference all weekend. I wasn't even in town on Friday. I can get you the hotel bill and my conference materials if you like."

Thanking her, you examine her receipts and the conference registration packet. Each indicates that she was out of town from Thursday through Monday.

"Before we get going, I have one more question, okay?"

"Sure, but just one. I have to get to class—my professor doesn't like us to be late."

"Thanks. . . . So, why didn't you report Dr. Myers missing when he didn't come in yesterday morning? Is it normal for him to stay home on Mondays?"

"Oh . . . no, I, uh . . . I didn't expect him back until next week. He, um, he e-mailed me . . . hold on, I'll print you a copy."

"Thanks." As Emily bounces off to Dr. Myers' computer, you realize Stransky has been very quietly blushing and staring at his shoes for the duration of the interview.

"Great," you mutter, "the rookie's got a crush on the co-ed."

Dr. Myers' e-mail states that he was taking the week off to spend time at home with his family. You enter this into evidence, along with Emily's receipts, being sure to affix and sign the proper chain-of-custody documentation.

Late Thursday evening, two Jacob's Falls teens happened upon a grisly scene. The decomposing body of a man later identified as Professor Kline was found lying supine along the banks of the creek. Since local weather conditions were quite warm all week, the level of decomposition and insect activity is extensive. Thus, the county medical examiner is left to rely on YOU, the State Police Forensic Entomologist, to determine the day and time the Professor died.

05:45 FRIDAY MAY 18—ARRIVAL AT THE SCENE: YOU BEGIN YOUR INVESTIGATION BY TAKING COPIOUS NOTES. THE FOLLOWING ITALICIZED PASSAGES ARE EXCERPTS FROM YOUR INVESTIGATOR'S NOTEBOOK

"A search of the scene reveals no shoe or footprints. I see no visible wounds on the body due to maggot activity and the advanced level of decomposition. Even so, there are no weapons in the area, or man-made items of any kind."

The silence of this painfully early morning is interrupted when one of the officers wonders out loud, "How did the Professor's body get to this area down here by the water? Was he carried? I don't see drag marks anywhere."

"A check of the weather report indicates that heavy downpours and flooding occurred all day Saturday and light rain fell on Tuesday night. This would obscure any footprints or tidemarks made at the time of the disappearance. A deputy has included a copy of the National Weather Service report for May 11 through present with the case file."

As the entomologist, you are obligated to reply, "Insect activity will reveal whether or not Professor Kline was in the water, and if so, how long ago he washed up onto his final resting place." You pause to record the location and time of the photos you are snapping. You take photos of the entire area, some of just the body, and some close-ups of the maggot-infested portions of the body.

"There is heavy maggot activity on and around Professor Kline's body, both feeding and migrating. The maggot mass is in his face and neck area. It appears that the soil around the body is undisturbed through the decomposition process. In addition, there is soil splashed up on the clothing as it would be during a rain storm. The body has likely been in this location since death or very soon thereafter."

As you collect maggot samples, you put some in jars filled with preservative. You label these with the date, time, location on the body, and your own initials. You also assign a unique number to each vial and record this in your notebook. Other maggots are put into fly-rearing chambers. These chambers are labeled in the same way. You will take these back to the lab to raise them to adulthood. This is the only way to positively identify the species colonizing poor Professor Kline.

In a clearing about 50 yards up the bank from Professor Kline's body, investigators find the dig site along with the Professor's vehicle.

> "The site is located on private property outside Jacob's Falls, which is an extremely rural and sparsely populated area of the state. The site consists of a 12 × 18 foot tarpaulin canopy that covers a 10 × 12 foot hole in the ground. It looks like the site was ransacked.

> "Maps, papers, water bottles, notebooks, photography equipment, and digging tools are strewn about the site. The cameras, papers, and notebooks have all been damaged by the rain. Two camping tents are 25 feet from the canopy, left open with their contents in disarray. It seems obvious that one belonged to each of the missing men. The fly, or waterproof overlay, from Professor Kline's tent is snagged on a tree a few yards away from the tent. One of the lines that connected it to the ground stake is missing.

> "The professor's vehicle is visible from the campsite. It is unlocked and everything appears to be in order. There is a conspicuous lack of evidence concerning Dr. Myers' vehicle, a Jeep Cherokee—it is nowhere to be found."

It is getting on into the breakfast hours and the deputies are starting to grumble about their collective hankering for some fresh coffee and pancakes. Over their complaints (and your own growling stomach) you can hear lots of vehicles and voices approaching.

The local media has reported the location of the site, no doubt lured by their police scanners and the State Police Helicopter performing an aerial search. By now, reporters, protestors, gold-diggers, and rubber-neckers alike are arriving in droves on what is rapidly becoming a very muggy morning. "Should have brought bug spray," you think, "but maybe that would damage my professional credibility?. . . I can see the headlines . . . 'Forensic Entomologist who Hates Bugs Investigating Disappearance.'" As you drift back to reality, you hear the crowd grow silent.

Steve Thompson, an environmental conservationist and self-proclaimed spokesman for the state forestlands, emerges from the crowd to speak to reporters. He is barking mad that the local residents were not consulted before Dr. Myers began his excavation, and he is calling for the prosecution of Dr. Myers and his team for destruction of state property. Aware that Thompson is an avid hunter and has detailed knowledge of the area, the police chief interviews him after the excitement dies down.

"Can you tell me your whereabouts for the last 7 days?" grunts the chief.

"I was in the company of my family," Mr. Thompson politely replies. He seems a little tense, and his eyes keep darting in your direction.

"I have been seen around town. Any of my friends will tell you I have done nothing out of the ordinary lately."

"So what you're saying is that you have no alibi?" says the chief.

"Right. . . . So what?"

CONCLUSIONS

You will need to use deductive reasoning to eliminate distracting information and stay focused on the elements of the crime! Hint: Keep a detective's notebook to write down your ideas as you go, keep a list of likely suspects, and establish a timeline of events. Include your calculations for the time of death and your conclusions concerning the most likely perpetrator. Don't be led astray—some witnesses may not be telling the truth!

Follow the clues and see if you can solve the mystery!

Prepare a case report outlining your findings and be able to back up your assertions with facts derived from the exercise. Include your answers to the following questions:

1. What is the timeline of events surrounding Professor Kline's disappearance and death?
2. What is the earliest possible time/date of Professor Kline's death?
3. Who do you think had the means to commit the crime?
4. Who had a motive?
5. What, if any, further information would help you with this case?

EVIDENCE REPORT

You have identified the species *Phormia regina* after examining the adults raised in the lab. Using the following you can calculate the shortest possible interval between the moment the first eggs were laid and the moment you collected the samples from the body.

ENTOMOLOGICAL EVIDENCE FROM PROFESSOR KLINE'S BODY

Maggot mass—neck region—all stages of *P. Regina* present, with migrating maggots present in the surrounding soil.

DATA TABLES

Time to Reach Life Cycle Stages—Black Blow Fly (measured in days)

Phormia regina

Temperature (°F)	65–up	50–65
Eggs	0.66	1.32
1st Instar Larvae	0.75	1.50
2nd Instar Larvae	0.46	0.92
3rd Instar Larvae	1.50	3.00
Migrating Maggots	3.50	7.00
Puparia	6.00	12.00
Total Days	12.88	25.76

National Weather Service Data for Cedar Creek

Date	Day	Sunrise	Sunset	Nighttime Temp (°F)	Daytime Temp (°F)
5/11	Friday	5:27	19:54	74	86
5/12	Saturday	5:26	19:55	62	70
5/13	Sunday	5:25	19:56	67	84
5/14	Monday	5:24	19:58	68	90
5/15	Tuesday	5:23	19:59	52	63
5/16	Wednesday	5:22	20:00	56	70
5/17	Thursday	5:21	20:01	68	72
5/18	Friday	5:20	20:02	69	86
5/19	Saturday	5:19	20:03	68	82
5/20	Sunday	5:18	20:04	71	88
5/21	Monday	5:18	20:05	72	91
5/22	Tuesday	5:17	20:06	65	85
5/23	Wednesday	5:16	20:06	67	84
5/24	Thursday	5:15	20:07	74	86
5/25	Friday	5:14	20:08	70	84

Email received by Emily, Dr. Myers' research assistant:

Delivered at 2:33 pm, Monday May 14, 2001

To: EMWils@allweb.net

From: digger222@cccc.edu

Subject: going home this week

Emily,
I will be spending next week at home with Jeannie and the kids.
Need some time at home.
See you next Monday.
Ralph

```
StayLong Motel
123 River Drive
Anytown, USA
888-555-1234


Receipt of Payment


3 nights @ $35.50/night
                    $106.50
Dbl occ.            $9.00

Subtotal            $115.50

Tax                 $7.99
                   _____
Total               $123.49

Charge: MC#xxxxxxx-2334


Cardholder Signature:

_____

Emily Wilson
```

May 23—Wednesday—Backpackers discovered a bloated body along a roadside trail about 10 miles from the dig site. A wallet found on the body identifies the man as Dr. Myers.

Flash Traffic on Police Radio:

A backpack has been found in a dumpster at the apartment complex where Emily Wilson resides. The backpack contains a rock hammer, the keys to a Jeep, a bloody man's button-down shirt, and what looks like a tent cord covered in blood.

Does this new case information affect your initial report?

Crime Scene Sketching and Digital Photography

CRIME SCENE SKETCHING

Before the jury hears testimony about the conditions at a crime scene, before blood evidence is collected for DNA analysis, before latent fingerprint development begins, even before the area around a body is combed for clues, the crime scene is documented by **sketching** and **photography**.

There are two phases to crime scene sketching—the **rough sketch** and the **finished sketch**. The most common view used in crime scene sketches is the *"bird's eye" view*. This is the view of the scene as from directly above, which does not include the appearance or contents of vertical surfaces like walls or cabinets. An *elevation* is the view from the side, and is always accompanied by the cardinal direction. For example, a particular view may be "the elevation of the north wall of the living room, Smith residence, 222 Mockingbird Lane, 1 January, 2001." The address, date, and your initials must be on each sketch, in addition to any other "chain-of-custody" documentation required by your instructor.

During the initial evaluation of the scene, an investigator must select two points of reference like "the north exterior wall" or a window or "the main entry door." These must be immovable, permanent features of the building or landscape. To generate a rough sketch, the investigator measures the dimensions of the space and uses these points to accurately characterize the contents of the scene. Major items of interest, like a body or a weapon, are located in reference to these points. For example, the investigator may select the south exterior wall of a home and the back door, located in the kitchen, as the two points of reference in a crime scene focused on the kitchen and stairs to the basement. The sketch should begin with the dimensions of the room(s) involved and the footprint of the dwelling, as well as the orientation of the building to due north, as it would appear on a map. The property surrounding the building, like the distance to a road, other buildings, or vehicles, may also be relevant to the investigation, so communication with the other investigators on scene is important during this portion of the crime scene analysis.

Once the floor plan of the building is documented, the specific contents are recorded. You must be sure to search the room in a methodical way, which is most commonly done by walking in a circle around the room, spiraling in toward the center. Furniture, blood spatter, bodies, weapons, and any other items of interest should be included on the drawing with the distance from each item to the two reference points determined earlier. It is not necessary to draw each item. Rather, a letter or number should be assigned to each and then included in the sketch. The appearance and orientation of these items are documented in the crime scene photographs and not on the sketch. Be sure to correlate the letter or number with the photographs as well.

Any details like odors, sounds, or other facts not encompassed by the sketch should be recorded in your investigator's notebook. The level of detail should be sufficient to adequately refresh your memory if you are called to testify in court. After the scene has been properly documented, a finished sketch is prepared in a controlled environment, like back in the lab or the office. It should be a neat version of the rough sketch clearly drawn to scale. Computer programs or printed cut-and-paste kits are also used by some law enforcement agencies to generate finished sketches.

MATERIALS

Sketch book (grid-ruled)
Pencil with eraser
Ruler

PROCEDURE

1. Generate a finished sketch from the rough sketch on page 16.[4]

---

[4] Courtesy Sirchie Fingerprint Laboratories, Inc., Youngsville, North Carolina.

CASE: 10-789-96
301 N. CENTRE ST.
OCT. 6, 1996   11:40 PM

HOMICIDE

VICTIM: LESTER W. BROWN
INVESTIGATOR: SGT. LA. DUFFY
ASS'T BY: PTLM. R.W. HICKS

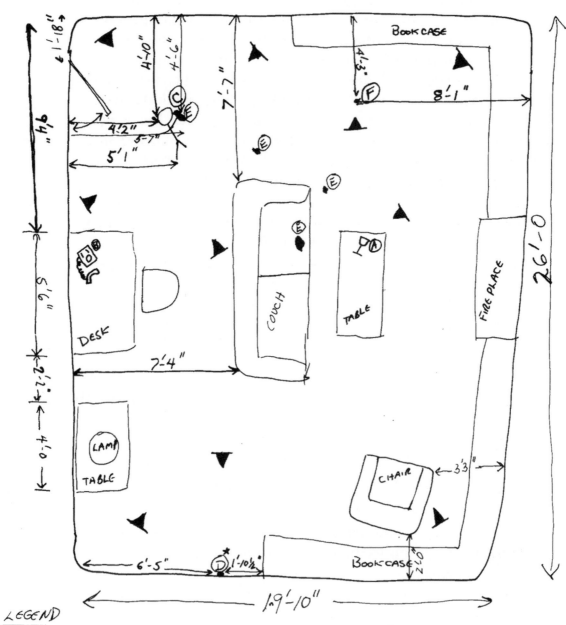

LEGEND

A = COCKTAIL GLASS
B = TELEPHONE
C = VICTIM
D = BULLET HOLE
E = BLOOD STAINS
F = SHELL CASING
▲ = CAMERA LOCATIONS

* D 3'-4¾" FROM FLOOR

¼" = 1 FOOT

2. It is necessary to draw the room to scale, meaning that the distances recorded in the rough sketch are in the same proportion in the finished sketch. This can be easily accomplished by using grid-ruled or graphing paper. Most grid-ruled paper is four squares per inch. For example, if you were to draw a room that is 12 feet by 18 feet, then you can make your drawing twelve squares by eighteen squares. This is a 1 foot = 1 square (or ¼ inch) scale. Sadly, this makes your drawing too small to be useful: only 3 inches by 4½ inches! This is remedied by increasing your scale to 1 foot = two squares (or ½ inch). This doubles the dimensions of your drawing to 6 inches by 9 inches, which will also adequately fill a standard size page. Consider the utility of a finished sketch: it will be entered into evidence and presented in court if the case goes to trial.

3. Note the location of any "evidence" you discover. Include these measurements in your sketch.

4. Indicate the length along each wall, as well as the exact location and size of items like sofas, chairs, and tables. Remember, your sketches will have to provide orientation within the crime scene to other investigators months and years from now—so make it as detailed and as accurate as time permits!

5. Your final sketch should correct any mistakes from the rough sketch. This gives you an opportunity to present a clean, clearly arranged diagram of the scene. Be sure to include the street address, date, and your name on each and every sketch generated during your investigation. Also include the items of evidence listed on the sketch and indicate the location using the assigned letter.

6. List the physical evidence you believe may be relevant to this investigation in the table following the sketch and make recommendations about how each should be tested (i.e., sent to the DNA laboratory, examined for trace evidence, dusted for latent fingerprints, collected and taken to the laboratory for tool mark or footprint comparison, etc.).

Item	Suggested Method of Analysis
_____	_____
_____	_____
_____	_____
_____	_____
_____	_____
_____	_____
_____	_____
_____	_____

FORENSIC PHOTOGRAPHY

The most important component of your forensic photography training is learning the features and functions specific to your camera. Naturally, these exercises could not be written for each make and model, so you will have to *read and understand the instruction manual provided with your camera!*

PHOTOGRAPHY IN CRIMINAL INVESTIGATIONS

Photographic documentation of physical evidence is necessary for several reasons:

1. A dispassionate and accurate description of the scene must be available to investigators for future analysis;
2. Biological evidence must be documented in its original condition for presentation in court, as this evidence is often altered during testing;
3. Physical evidence must be presented in the context in which it was found; and
4. The adage that "a picture tells a thousand words" is especially true in forensic science.

Various techniques must be employed to accurately photograph the myriad circumstances that arise at crime scenes. Personal items, dwellings, and landscapes may be present at one time, and the proficient forensic photographer is required to preserve these scenes exactly as they are.

Understanding the basic features of your camera will enable you to solve problems on scene, providing fewer delays in the investigation. However, it is never advisable to rush through a scene. Take your time and plan your photographs before you make them.

PHOTOGRAPHY BASICS

A digital photograph is made when a light-sensing microchip inside the camera is exposed to light coming from the object or scene you wish to capture. The microchip is kept in the dark by the **shutter**, which is opened when you depress the shutter button to take the picture. This creates the characteristic noise you hear when taking a picture with a film camera.

The duration of exposure can be adjusted to suit the level of ambient light: **shutter speed** is measured in seconds, or fractions of seconds. If your camera has this feature, manual shutter speed can be set to 2, 1, 1/4, 1/8, 1/250, and 1/500 seconds. This may seem like an impossibly short span of time, but a whole second is actually considered a long exposure. This feature is important if you must capture action in crisp focus, like a 100-meter sprinter. For this application, your shutter speed must be very short, like 1/500. A long exposure may be required for extremely low light conditions, but necessitates the use of a tripod to keep the camera from moving. Most forensic evidence is inanimate, making shutter speed manipulation less common.

Another way to control the amount of light entering the camera is through the size of the opening itself, or the **aperture**. This describes the width of the hole in the lens, and controls the amount of light sent though the lens to the sensor. The measure of aperture diameter is not expressed in inches or centimeters. Rather, it is expressed as a fraction (**f/number**) of the size of the aperture relative to the focal length (discussed below) of the lens.

Standard f/number settings have come to be known as **stops**, along a continuous range of possible aperture sizes. For example, the lowest f/number (f/number 1.0) is arbitrarily designated as **f/stop** zero, or f/0. Each f/stop represents a two-fold difference in the amount of light entering the camera. The confusing part is that f/2 provides a *larger* aperture than f/7. For the sake of standardization within the photography industry, some f/stops are preset in your camera. These are numbered in order of decreasing aperture. Thus, f/3 provides twice as much light as f/4, which provides twice as much light as f/5, and so on.

Digital cameras designed for the casual user rely on preprogrammed settings and computer technology to determine the optimal settings (like shutter speed, f/stop, etc.) for each photograph you take. In place of manual f/stop operation, **exposure compensation**, or **exposure value (EV) adjustment**, may be used to capture an extremely bright or dark image. Most cameras offer values ranging from −2, −1, 0, 1, and 2. The "0" setting refers to your starting point—that is, the conditions which the camera's autofocus feature determined to be optimal. Adjusting toward negative numbers will reduce the exposure, thereby darkening a bright (overexposed) shot.

For an outdoor scene or a landscape, you will need to select a small aperture, like f/7. A portrait would require a large aperture, like f/2. This is determined by the requirements for the **depth of field**, which is most important in close-up work. The depth of field describes the portion of the area in front of you that is captured in sharp focus by the camera. You can demonstrate this idea with a microscope. As you increase your magnification, the actual amount of sample visible through the eyepiece is reduced.

Do not confuse the digital zoom feature of your camera with an actual zoom lens. The **zoom lens** is either attached to or part of the end of the lens outside the body of the camera. A **digital zoom** feature is the preprogrammed capability of the built-in camera software to isolate a portion of an image and increase its size relative to the viewing screen. The power of a digital zoom is commensurate with the resolution available in the chip. A 6 megapixel (MP, meaning million pixels) camera would produce a more detailed digital zoom than would a 2MP camera. **Resolution** is also directly related to the number of pixels available to capture the image. As with zoom, the greater the number of pixels, the better the resolution.

Flash photography is a skill which demands time and practice to master. It is important to know how to adjust your flash for specific lighting conditions and working distance; however, the autosensors in digital cameras do an excellent job with a few exceptions. When making a photograph up close, it is necessary to reduce flash intensity to avoid overexposure. The **working distance** is the distance between your lens and the object you are photographing, and short working distance requires more care and planning for the use of your flash. Digital cameras simply cannot react quickly enough to capture a clear image at a short working distance. Consult your owner's manual on how to manually adjust the flash on your digital camera.

A **photograph log** is a running list of the photos you take at a scene, and the order in which they were taken. *This is essential and non-negotiable*! Keep a photograph log in your laboratory notebook so you can clearly identify the subject, location, and time. Be sure to record the setting on your camera used to create each image. The best way to learn the performance and features specific to your model of camera is to record your settings and evaluate the image at your desktop computer. This way, when a similar situation arises in the future, you will be prepared with the optimal settings for your camera.

EXERCISE 1 – FOCUS CONTROL

Please note: *Your digital camera may not allow you to change the point of focus.*

Digital cameras designed for the casual user rely on preprogrammed settings and computer technology to determine the optimal settings (like shutter speed, f/stop, etc.) for each photograph you take. Only professional quality digital cameras allow you to manually adjust the f/stop, but the same result can be roughly obtained with one of these three settings:

Macro mode, for shots a few inches away, extreme close-ups;

Portrait mode, for objects 10 to 20 feet away; and

Landscape (a.k.a. Infinity) mode, which is best for photographing scenery or distant, sweeping views.

For this exercise, you will need to take your camera, your laboratory exercise textbook, and your lab partner outdoors.

1. Position your lab partner (now your subject), laboratory textbook in hand, with an expanse of field or parking lot in the background.
2. Step back from your subject approximately 4 feet. Ask your lab partner to hold your laboratory textbook straight out with both hands, making sure his/her face is still in view. This should set the scene with the textbook about 18 inches from the camera, the subject's face about 4 feet away, and the scenery off in the distance.
3. With the camera set on portrait mode, autofocus on your subject's face and take a photograph.
4. Change the camera to macro mode and take a picture. You should see the textbook has come into clearer focus.
5. Change the camera to landscape mode and take a third picture. You should find both your subject and the textbook are out of focus. This demonstrates changes in depth of field as the camera has automatically adjusted the f/stop and shutter speed relative to the preprogrammed settings.

EXERCISE 2 – COPING WITH BACKLIGHTING

Please note: Your digital camera may not allow you to change the point of focus.

Begin with your camera in the automatic/autofocus mode. Set up your subject indoors.

1. Select a subject, like your lab partner, and seat him/her by a table with a window behind your subject.
2. Seat yourself about 3 feet from your subject and take a picture. This has likely produced a very bright, washed-out image with your subject's face in shadow.
3. Next, adjust the exposure compensation, or EV adjustment, to correct the overexposed image.
4. Retake the same picture. Has the quality of the image been improved?
5. If necessary, readjust the exposure control and retake the picture.

If your camera offers it, the best setting to fix this problem is known as center-weighted or spot metering. Center-weighted metering directs the camera to determine the optimal settings based on the light conditions present in the center of the field (around your subject's face). Spot metering directs the camera to calculate the best settings for the light conditions in the center of the viewfinder. The default setting, called matrix or evaluative metering, is based on the average light intensity across the entire field of view.

Some manufacturers have preprogrammed settings named for specific light conditions and composition. You may find, for example, a setting for taking a portrait with bright backlighting. This feature is similar to the center-weighted metering and will work in the same way. Here again, it is essential to explore the features specific to your camera.

EXERCISE 3 – CONSTRUCTING A PANORAMIC VIEW
MATERIALS

Digital camera on automatic mode (Your camera may offer a "panoramic" or "panorama assist" mode.
Follow the manufacturer's instructions for using this feature.)
Interior room

PROCEDURE

1. Take your first photograph where you would naturally enter. Be sure to include the floor in the frame as a reference.

2. Continue snapping photos while walking around the room, overlapping them slightly. It is a good idea to be methodical in your coverage, perhaps working from left to right, floor to ceiling. You are simply documenting the scene, so no single piece of evidence should be photographed in detail.

3. Back at the lab, print out your photos. Arrange them in a panoramic view of the room by overlapping them and pinning them to a bulletin or poster board.

4. Alternately, you can accomplish this same result using digital image processing software.

EXERCISE 4 – DOCUMENTING EVIDENCE

MATERIALS

Digital camera on automatic mode

Interior room with three objects (i.e., items of evidence)

    An object flat on the floor, like a ransom note or shoeprint;

    A thick object lying flat on a table, like a book; and

    An object flat to the wall, like a handprint or blood spatter.

Metric ruler

PROCEDURE

You will photograph each item three times. Be sure to record the sequence and camera settings in your photograph log.

    You can see how this is done on the web. Go to http://www.sccja.org/csr-photosequence.htm.

OBJECT A

1. Take one photograph at a distance of 6 feet, to orient the object in the room.

2. Take a second photograph of the object up close, with a centimeter or two of the substrate bordering it. The object should fill up the frame. Stand *directly* above the object, so your camera is parallel with the plane of the floor.

3. Take a third photograph just like the second, but this time include your ruler (known as scale) next to the object. Since object A is flat on the floor, you need only lay the ruler down next to it. Be sure to orient the camera at 90° to the wall, as the scale will be useless otherwise!

OBJECT B

1. Take the first photograph from several feet away, to establish the orientation of the object in the room.
2. Take the second photograph up close, without scale. Be sure to angle the camera so it is 90° from the plane of the object (i.e., perpendicular to it).
3. Take the third photograph with scale. The trick is to photograph the ruler at the same height as the top-most plane of the object. One method is to keep a handful of pennies in your kit and arrange two stacks of the required height adjacent to the object. Place the ruler on top and photograph the item with a small border of background. Be sure to orient the camera at 90° to the wall, as the scale will be useless otherwise!

OBJECT C

1. Take the first photograph from several feet away, to establish its orientation in the room.
2. Take the second photograph up close, without scale. Remember to hold the camera at 90° from the wall.
3. Take the third photograph as before, using your lab partner to hold the ruler next to the object. An alternative to this is to use adhesive tape rulers, available from a forensic or crime scene response supply house. Be sure to orient the camera at 90° to the wall, as the scale will be useless otherwise!

Forensic Glass Analysis

Glass analysis is a useful tool for a forensic scientist. Analysis may include examining glass fragments to determine the direction of impact which will show from which side a window may have been broken. It may also include examining glass and determining its density or refractive index in an attempt to identify the type of glass, for example, from a car headlight or from a window pane.

Glass is manufactured in different ways and for different purposes. Typical examples include:

- **Soda-lime-silicate glass.** This is most commonly used for flat glass, bottles, containers, and light bulbs.
- **Borosilicate glass.** This has a higher resistance to acid corrosion and is typically used for car headlights, Pyrex®, thermometers, and laboratory glassware.
- **Alumino-silicate glass.** This is more thermal resistant and is used in laboratory glassware, glass fibers, and stove-top cookware.
- **Lead-alkali-silicate glass.** More commonly known as lead crystal, this is used for decorative glassware and neon signs.

EXERCISE 1 – DISPLACEMENT OF WATER

SAFETY

MATERIALS

Aluminum bars of varying length (density = 2.70 g/cm^3)
Balance
100-mL graduated cylinder
Water

PROCEDURE

1. Measure the mass of each aluminum bar according to the protocol provided by your instructor. Record the mass to the nearest 0.01 g.

2. Fill the graduated cylinder to a level of your choice. Be sure to read the volume at the lowest point of the curve (meniscus) at the surface of the water. Record this in your notebook.

3. Place the aluminum bar into the graduated cylinder by tying a string around it and lowering it carefully so that it is completely submerged.

4. Read the new level of the meniscus and record this volume in your notebook.

5. Subtract the first volume from the second volume, and record this as the volume of the aluminum bar. This is known as the **water displacement method** of density determination.

   Remember that: **1 mL = 1 cm^3**

   This means that the volume of water displaced by the aluminum bar in milliliters (mL) is equal to the volume in cubic centimeters (cm^3).

6. Divide the weight of the bar by its volume to calculate the density.

7. Repeat these measurements for a number of bars of varying length and record your results.

8. How close did you come to calculating the known density of aluminum (2.70 g/cm^3)?

EXERCISE 2 – COMPARING GLASS DENSITY[5, 6]

Glass density can be easily determined by measuring the mass and volume of a sample, as demonstrated in Exercise 1. However, in many cases the amount of evidence is so small that it is too difficult to measure mass and volume accurately. In this situation, the density of a glass fragment can be measured indirectly by determining in which liquid of known density the sample becomes suspended.

SAFETY

MATERIALS

Glass samples (for example, glass from different sources: household windows, borosilicate/Pyrex®, tempered/safety glass, food containers)

10-mL graduated cylinder

Water

Sodium polytungstate (aq) solution (density 2.8–3.0 g/mL) in a dropper bottle[6]

PROCEDURE

Part I

There are three types of glass samples available for testing:

a. Sample "a" is from a crime scene.
b. Sample "b" was found embedded in the shoe of suspect #1.
c. Sample "c" was found embedded in the shoe of suspect #2.

1. Add 5 mL of distilled water to a 10 mL graduated cylinder.
2. Add sample "a" to the water.
3. Add 1-mL increments of sodium polytungstate solution to the sample.
4. After each addition, swirl the cylinder gently to mix. Observe the glass chip.

---

[5] Courtesy of Joanne Long, Faculty of Cherry Hill High School East, Cherry Hill, New Jersey.

[6] Please refer to the *Instructor's Manual* for additional preparation instructions relating to this experiment.

5. Continue adding until the chip becomes suspended in the solution, somewhere in the middle.
6. Now add the glass fragment from suspect #1. Allow it to equilibrate.
7. Repeat for the sample from suspect #2.

If glass chips stay suspended in the liquid for at least 1 minute, they compare by density. If only the crime scene glass sample remains suspended, while the questioned sample either sinks to the bottom or rises to the top, then the samples do not compare by density. Outline your findings.

Part II

If your sample is large enough the direct measurement of density can be done as follows:

1. Place your crime scene sample onto a balance and record the mass to the nearest 0.01 g.
2. Repeat for each of the suspect samples.
3. Record the values in the table below on page 29.
4. Fill a 50-mL beaker half full and place it on the balance. Tare the balance.
5. Attach a piece of thread to your crime scene sample and carefully lower it into the beaker of water. It should not touch the sides or bottom of the beaker.
6. Record the mass, which is the mass of water displaced by the glass.
7. Repeat steps 4–6 for each suspect sample.

Water has a density of 1 g/mL, which means that 1 g of water occupies a volume of 1 mL.

Using the mass of water displaced, calculate the volume of water displaced for the crime scene sample and the suspect samples.

This volume must be the same as the volume of each glass sample. Record the volumes for each sample in the table.

Now calculate the density of each using the formula:

Density = mass ÷ volume

Figure 1   Radial cracks in a pane of glass. *Courtesy Sirchie Fingerprint Laboratories, Inc, Youngsville, North Corolina.*

Sample	Mass (g)	Mass H₂0 Displaced (g)	Volume (mL)	Density (g/mL)
Crime scene				
Suspect #1				
Suspect #2				

Some typical density values expected would be:

Lead-alkali silicate (lead crystal)—2.65–3.0 g/mL
Soda-lime silicate (flat glass)—2.41–2.63 g/mL
Auto glass (not headlights)—2.53–2.75 g/mL
Pyrex®—2.26–2.39 g/mL
Borosilicate (car headlights)—2.20–2.29

EXERCISE 3 – GLASS FRACTURE ANALYSIS

When sufficient force is applied to a piece of glass it will break. The initial point at which it breaks is known as a **radial fracture**. As the glass moves outward secondary breaks appear known as **tangential fractures** (see Figure 2).

SAFETY

MATERIALS

Glass pane(s)
Marker
Two 3-inch lengths of lumber
Cardboard box
Hammer
Hand lens

PROCEDURE

1. Take a small pane of glass and, using a marker pen, draw a picture on one side.
2. Place the pane, with the picture side uppermost, onto two raised wood blocks inside a cardboard box. Place a safety screen in front.
3. Wearing safety goggles, press down on the middle of the glass using a small hammer. You may need to apply more force than you think.
4. Once it is broken, remove the glass fragments from the cardboard box and carefully reconstruct the glass pane at your bench.
5. Take one of the larger broken pieces and examine the edges with a hand lens. Try to determine the direction of the force using **the 3R rule**:

The ridges on Radial cracks are at Right angles to the Rear.

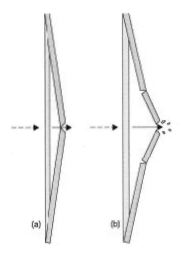

Figure 2   Diagram of the production of radial and concentric cracks in glass. Note how radial cracks are formed first (a) from the side opposite the direction of force. Next, concentric cracks form (b) on the same side as the force.

Figure 3   View of the edge of a radial crack in a piece of glass. Arrow indicates direction of force.

Fingerprinting

CASE HISTORY

The Night Stalker Murders

Richard Ramirez committed his first murder in June, 1984. His victim was a 79-year-old woman who was stabbed repeatedly, sexually assaulted, and then had her throat slashed. It would be 8 months before Ramirez murdered again. In the spring, Ramirez began a murderous rampage which ultimately resulted in thirteen additional killings and five rapes. His *modus operandi* was to enter a home through an open window, shoot the male residents, and savagely rape his female victims. He scribed a pentagram on the wall of one of his victims and the words "Jack the Knife," and was reported by another to force her to "swear to Satan" during the assault. His identity still unknown, the news media dubbed him the "Night Stalker" as the body count continued to rise. Public hysteria and a media frenzy prevailed.

The break in the case came when the license plate of what seemed to be a suspicious car relating to a sighting of the Night Stalker was reported to the police. The police determined that the car had been stolen and eventually located it, abandoned in a parking lot. After processing the car for prints, they found one usable partial fingerprint. This fingerprint was entered into LAPD's brand-new AFIS computerized fingerprint system. Without AFIS, it would have taken a single technician, manually searching the Los Angeles' 1.7 million print cards, 67 years to come up with the perpetrator's prints. The Night Stalker was identified as Richard Ramirez, who had been fingerprinted following a traffic violation some years before. Police searching the home of one of his friends found the gun used to commit the murders, and jewelry belonging to his victims was found in the possession of Ramirez's sister. Ramirez was convicted of murder and sentenced to death in 1989.

INTRODUCTION

On the surface of your fingertips are raised lines called friction ridges. Along the top edge of these ridges are pores that secrete sweat, a mixture of salt, proteins, and water. When you touch something—like when drinking from a glass, selecting a compact disc, or closing a car door—you leave behind a print of the pattern on your fingertip. In 1880, Francois Galton recognized that these ridge patterns are different from person to person, and determined that these "fingerprints" can be used as a means of personal identification. His work is the basis for our current system of fingerprint classification.

Since the late nineteenth century, the science of fingerprinting has come a long way. There are two distinct skill sets in the field of fingerprint analysis: classification and development. An important distinction to grasp is the difference between inked and latent fingerprints. Inked prints are collected directly from an individual's hand. Latent prints are developed on a surface, documented via photographs, and lifted via varying techniques.

The individuality of a fingerprint is not determined by its general shape or pattern but by a careful study of its **ridge characteristics** (also known as **minutiae**). It is the identity, number, and relative location of characteristics, such as those illustrated in Figure 1, that impart individuality to a fingerprint. If two prints are to compare, they will have to reveal characteristics that not only are identical but have the same relative location to one another in a print. In a judicial proceeding, a point-by-point comparison must be demonstrated by the expert.

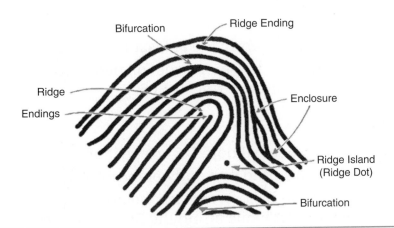

Figure 1   Fingerprint ridge characteristics.

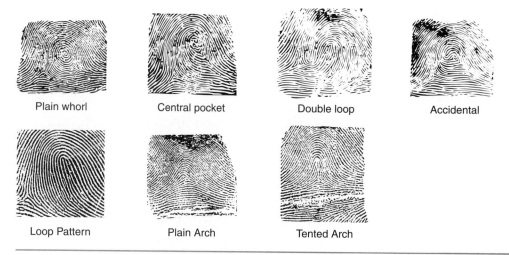

Figure 2   Loop, whorl, and arch fingerprint patterns.

All fingerprints are divided into three classes on the basis of their general pattern: **loops, whorls,** and **arches.** Sixty to 65 percent of the population has loops, 30 to 35 percent has whorls, and about 5 percent has arches. These three classes form the basis for all ten-finger classification systems presently in use. Whorls are actually divided into four distinct groups, as shown in Figure 2: plain, central pocket loop, double loop, and accidental. Arches, the least common of the three general patterns, are subdivided into two distinct groups: plain arches and tented arches.

CLASSIFICATION OF FINGERPRINTS

EXERCISE 1 – BALLOON PRINTS

MATERIALS

White latex balloons—provide at least three per student
Fingerprinting pad—thermoplastic ink pad is suggested, available through Sirchie, Cat # PFP602

PROCEDURE

1. Partially inflate a balloon. Do not tie it off.
2. Open fingerprinting pad and gently roll one fingertip.
3. Apply finger to balloon surface, being careful not to smudge or twist while lifting the finger from the balloon surface.

4. Inflate balloon enough to view expanded details of the print. Is the print an arch, loop, or whorl?

5. Examine print for quality and resolution of ridge detail. Repeat printing procedure if necessary.

6. Draw a simple diagram of print in your notebook, indicating ridge detail and minutiae found in enlarged fingerprint.

7. Be sure to indicate which hand and finger you printed!

EXERCISE 2 – GRAPHITE PRINTS

MATERIALS

Graphite pencil—HB or softer

Notebook paper

Transparent tape—1-inch wide invisible (gift-wrapping) tape is recommended

PROCEDURE*

1. Use a pencil to mark a 2-inch square on a sheet of notebook paper. Hold the pencil at an angle so that the side of the pencil point is flat to the paper.

2. Fill the square with graphite until it is shiny.

3. Roll the tip of one finger over the shiny graphite square, making one or two passes. Good technique demands including the entire fingertip, edge to edge and down to the area of the first joint (the wrinkled lines).

4. A lab partner should then pull a 2–3 inch length of transparent tape, touching the ends only, and present it sticky-side up.

5. Roll your graphite-covered fingertip onto the tape, covering as much of the graphite area as possible.

6. Carefully peel off the tape and affix it where indicated in the following squares.

7. Repeat this process for each finger of one hand.

8. If these steps do not yield a good print, it may be because the fingertip is too dry. Rubbing your fingers through your hair or on your forehead to pick up oils should solve the problem. Then repeat the previous procedure.

*This same procedure can be performed with chalk dust on black paper. Construction paper is not recommended. Rather, a photocopier can be used to make black sheets by "copying" with the lid open and no document on the tray.

NAME _____

R Thumb	R Index	R Middle	R Ring	R Little
L Thumb	L Index	L Middle	L Ring	L Little

EXERCISE 3 – INKED PRINTS

MATERIALS

Fingerprinting pad—thermoplastic ink pad is suggested, available through Sirchie, Cat # PIP601 or PFP602
Plain white paper

PROCEDURE

1. On a sheet of scrap paper, practice rolling your lab partner's prints.
2. Cover your partner's finger with a thin coat of ink from the crease at the first knuckle to the very top.
3. When rolling onto the paper, make one pass in a smooth, even motion. Roll nailbed to nailbed. Do not roll back and forth!
4. When you feel comfortable with your technique, roll a full set of prints onto the following squares. Be sure that both you and your partner wash your hands before beginning the final version.
5. Roll each finger, one at a time, onto the inked print data sheet. Your instructor may provide you with photocopies of this sheet in lieu of removing the page from your book.
6. Allow the sheet to dry before affixing it into your laboratory notebook.

NAME _____

R Thumb	R Index	R Middle	R Ring	R Little
L Thumb	L Index	L Middle	L Ring	L Little

EXERCISE 4 – FINGERPRINT COMPARISON AND CLASSIFICATION

MATERIALS

Prints generated from previous exercise

Magnifying lens

PROCEDURE

1. Using your own prints, classify them into major groups (loop, arch, whorl), and describe minutiae.
2. Label at least five points of comparison for each print.
3. Prepare a report outlining the classification and the five points of comparison for each print.

DEVELOPING LATENT FINGERPRINTS

EXERCISE 1 – IODINE FUMING

SAFETY

SUPPLIES

Plain white index card

Fuming chamber—"Insta-FumeTent™" is suggested, available through Sirchie, Cat # FR150

Iodine crystals, available thorough Sirchie Cat # A211C

Watchglass

Mug warmer or hotplate, available through Sirchie, Cat # FHP100

PROCEDURE

1. Rub your fingers through your hair, on your forehead, or behind your ear to pick up oils.
2. Place a fingerprint on the center of the index card. Label the edge of the card with your name/date.
3. Hang the card by the name/date end with the clips provided with the Insta-FumeTent™.
4. Inside the fuming chamber, arrange a mug warmer or hotplate with a watchglass or other heatproof vessel on top. Add approximately two dozen iodine crystals to the watchglass.
5. Close the fuming chamber.
6. Turn on the hotplate to a low setting.
7. Carefully monitor the development of the prints.
8. Do not overdevelop! Applying too much iodine can permanently discolor the paper, destroying the print. Careful attention and practice is required to develop a usable fingerprint.

EXERCISE 2 – FINGERPRINT POWDER

SAFETY

MATERIALS

Black fingerprint powder, available through Sirchie, Cat # 101L

Fiberglass fingerprinting brush, availbale through Sirchie, Cat #122L

1-inch wide transparent tape

Smooth, shiny object, light in color

PROCEDURE

1. Apply a fingerprint, in the manner previously described, to a light-colored shiny (nonporous) object like a compact disc, soda can, or glass microscope slide.

2. Apply fingerprint powder with a fiberglass fingerprint brush. Be sure to use the brush with its companion powder—never interchange brushes with multiple powder colors!

3. Tap or twist excess powder from the bristles into the lid of its container.

4. Dip the brush into powder. It is poor technique to overload the brush, forcing the powder up into the base of the bristles. This makes it difficult to control the amount of powder deposited on the surface to be dusted, which can easily ruin a very clearly defined latent print.

5. Using a circular pattern, swirl the brush over the print. The bristles should just graze the surface of the object. The print should begin to appear.

6. It may be necessary to go back for more powder to complete the development.

7. Remember, it is better to quit while you are ahead than ruin your print and have to start again! Do not overapply your powder.

8. It may take several tries to produce quality prints.

9. Lift prints with transparent tape and apply to the work-sheet following this exercise.

EXERCISE 3 – SUPERGLUE® FUMING OF SMALL ITEMS

SAFETY

MATERIALS

Superglue®
Glass microscope slide
60-mm plastic (disposable) culture dish
Mug warmer (or in home heating pad)
Water, in a dropper bottle

In this exercise you will develop a latent fingerprint with Superglue® in a culture dish.

PROCEDURE

1. Place a fingerprint on the end of a glass microscope slide. *Do not* rub your fingertip along your nose or through your hair before you apply the print—if the print you deposit is easily seen, then you must start over with a less oily finger. Overloading will produce an obscured and overdeveloped print.
2. Label the other end of the slide with your name and the date.
3. Place the bottom of a culture dish on the heating pad. Turn the heating pad on to a medium setting. It is okay if the dish is not absolutely level.
4. Place a penny or poker chip in the center of a culture dish.
5. Place the slide with the fingerprinted side facing up on top of it.
6. Add a few drops of Superglue® to the dish (in the low end, if applicable). Do not get any on the slide itself.
7. Add one drop of water to the opposite side of the dish. Do not put any water on the slide itself.
8. Immediately apply the culture dish lid.
9. Observe the progress of the fuming and remove the lid when the print appears completely developed. Be careful to keep your face away from the dish while you are opening it—acrylic vapors are irritating to nasal membranes.
10. Remove the slide from the dish and examine your fingerprint. The ridge pattern should appear white.
11. You may wish to dust the print with black powder to improve the contrast of the print against the background.
12. Tape your slide to your notebook and include it with your laboratory report.

Courtesy Sirchie Fingerprint Laboratories, Inc., Youngsville, North Carolina.

EXERCISE 4 – SUPERGLUE FUMING OF LARGE ITEMS

SAFETY

MATERIALS

Empty soda can

Fuming chamber—"Insta-FumeTent™" is suggested, available through Sirchie, Cat # FR150

Superglue®

Water

Two foil trays, available through Sirchie, Cat # CNA106

Mug warmer or hotplate, available through Sirchie, Cat # FHP100

In this exercise you will develop a latent fingerprint with Superglue® in a tent made of plastic sheeting.

PROCEDURE

1. Rub your fingers through your hair, on your forehead, or behind your ear to pick up oils.
2. Place a fingerprint on an empty aluminum soda can. Label the can with your name and date.
3. Place the can in the center of the fuming chamber. The chamber should be inside a fume hood (with the vent running).
4. Inside the fuming chamber, arrange a foil tray on top of the mug warmer/hotplate. Add approximately five drops of Superglue®. Place a foil tray of water on the mug warmer. This will enhance the activity of the Superglue® vapors.
5. Close the fuming chamber and turn on the hotplate to a low setting.
6. Carefully monitor the development of the prints—development times will vary. You may see white wisps of cyanoacrylate vapors rising from the foil tray.
7. Open the fuming chamber with the hood vent running. Superglue® vapors are noxious and can irritate mucous membranes—exercise safety precautions!
8. Remove your item carefully. *Do not touch the print!*
9. You may wish to dust the print with black powder to improve the contrast of the print against the background.
10. If possible, photograph your print (with scale) and include this in your report. Indicate specific locations of unique ridge details.

The Microscope[7]

CASE HISTORY

Sacco and Vanzetti

In 1920, two security guards were viciously gunned down by unidentified assailants. The security guards were transporting shoe factory payroll, nearly $16,000.00 in cash, at the time of the robbery-murder. Eyewitnesses described the assailants as "Italian-looking," one with a full handle-bar moustache. The robbers had used two firearms, leaving behind three different brands of shells.

Two suspects were identified and arrested, Nicola Sacco and his friend, the amply mustachioed Bartolomeo Vanzetti. After denying owning any firearms, each was found to be in possession of a loaded pistol. In fact, Sacco's pistol was a .32 caliber, the same caliber as the crime scene bullets. Sacco's pockets contained twenty-three bullets matching the brands of the empty shells found at the murder scene.

This case coincided with the "Red Scare," a politically turbulent time in post-World War I America. Citizens feared socialist zealots and the media played up these emotions. Political maneuvering and the use of the media muddied the waters surrounding the case, and the fact that both suspects were members of anarchist political groups that advocated revolutionary violence against the government only incited public animosity toward them. Sympathetic socialist organizations attempted to turn Sacco and Vanzetti into martyrs, calling their prosecution a "witch hunt."

The outcome of the trial ultimately depended on whether the prosecution was able to prove that Sacco's pistol fired the

---

[7] Please refer to the *Instructor's Manual for Criminalistics,* 9th edition for additional preparation instructions relating to this experiment.

bullets that killed the two security guards. At trial, the ballistic experts testified that the bullets used were no longer in production and they could not find similar ammunition to use in test firings—aside from the unused cartridges found in Sacco's pockets. A forensic expert for the prosecution concluded that a visual examination showed that the bullets matched, leading the jury to return a verdict of guilty. Sacco and Vanzetti were sentenced to death.

Because of continued public protests, a committee was appointed in 1927 to review the case. Around this time, Calvin Goddard, at the Bureau of Forensic Ballistics in New York, perfected the comparison microscope for use in forensic firearm investigations. With this instrument, two bullets are viewed side-by-side to compare the striations imparted to a bullet's surface as it travels through the gun's barrel. The committee asked Goddard to examine the bullets in question. A test-fired bullet from Sacco's weapon was matched conclusively by Goddard to one of the crime scene bullets. The fates of Sacco and Vanzetti were sealed and they were put to death in 1927.

INTRODUCTION

In 1590, Zacharias Janssen paired the first set of compound lenses and is credited with inventing the compound microscope. Centuries later the microscope remains the most important instrument in the service of science, especially forensic science.

Handling a microscope is best described as a habit; some are good and some are bad. Proper use of the features and careful maintenance of the components are essential, and will provide a scientist with reliable results. Disregard these instructions to your peril.

Always start with the lowest power objective, never with the highest! In turn, begin adjusting your focus with the coarse adjustment knob, and finish with the fine adjustment. The exception to this rule is this: use ONLY the fine adjustment knob with high-power magnification!

For the stereoscopic microscope, a special set of circumstances will apply: identify which of the two eyepieces has a focus adjustment ring. If the adjustable eyepiece is on your left, begin by closing your left eye. Now, bring your object into focus using the previous method while looking through your right eye. Once you can see clearly, switch to the other eye and *adjust the focus by using the ring on the eyepiece*. Do not touch the coarse or

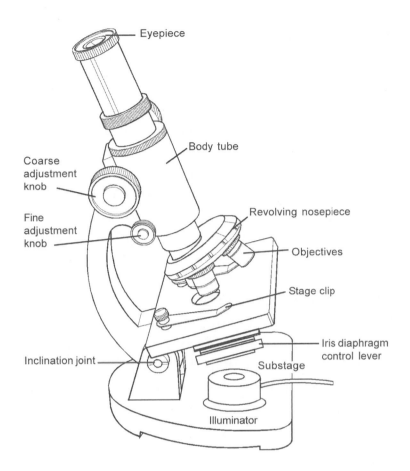

fine adjustment knobs at the base of the microscope! Once the view in your left eye is in perfect focus, close both and look away for a moment. When you come back, your stereoscopic microscope should be perfectly adjusted for your eyes only!

EXERCISE 1 – EXAMINATION OF EVIDENCE USING THE COMPOUND MICROSCOPE

SAFETY

MATERIALS

Glass microscope slides and coverslips
Small newspaper clippings
Water, in a dropper bottle
Straight edge blade or small scissors
Forceps
Compound microscope

PROCEDURE

Part I

1. Cut a lowercase letter "e" from your newspaper clipping. Place it on a slide, near the center.
2. Apply a drop of water on top of the "e" to make a wet-mount.
3. Apply a coverslip by holding it with one edge touching the slide at a 45° angle on the side of the drop of water.
4. Lower the coverslip onto the water, leaving the "e" centered.
5. Put the slide on the stage and clamp down. Note the orientation of the letter relative to you—is it right side up?
6. View the "e" under 100× magnification. Begin with the coarse adjustment and bring the "e" into sharp focus. Is the "e" still right side up?
7. Position the "e" so it is over the middle of the hole in the stage using your stage micrometer. When the stage is moved to the right, which direction does the "e" move?
8. Practice moving the "e" up and down and right to left, demonstrating **translational movement** of the image.
9. View under 200× magnification, bringing the "e" into focus *with the fine adjustment only*. Notice that a smaller portion of the slide is visible under the higher magnification. This demonstrates the reduction of the **field of view** with increased magnification power. Also note that the distance between the objective and slide decreases when switching from lower to higher magnification, which is called a reduction in the **working distance**. Care must be taken to avoid engaging an objective that will damage a microscope slide. It is for this reason that only the fine adjustment is used to focus when using high-power magnification.
10. Once you bring the top surface of the "e" into focus, turn the fine adjustment knob a little bit in both directions while looking through the eyepiece. Notice how you are able to focus at varying distances through the paper. This demonstrates the **depth of focus** through the thickness of your specimen.

EXERCISE 2 – EXAMINATION OF EVIDENCE USING THE STEREOSCOPIC MICROSCOPE

PART I EXAMINATION OF VEGETATION

SAFETY

MATERIALS

> Dried oregano or catnip
> Forceps
> Glass microscope slides
> Coverslips
> Stereoscopic microscope

PROCEDURE

1. Put a few pieces of dried herb on a slide and apply a coverslip.
2. Position the sample in the center of your field of view.
3. Examine the vegetation through the depth of focus. Is this useful in your characterization of this material? Note the tremendous depth of field the stereoscopic microscope provides, allowing for a three-dimensional examination of the vegetation.

PART II EXAMINATION OF TYPEFACE

1. Examine the "e" you prepared in the previous exercise.
2. Use the clamp to affix the slide to the stage. Note the orientation of the letter relative to you—make sure it is right side up before you look through the eyepiece.
3. Position the "e" so it is over the middle of the hole in the stage using your stage micrometer.

4. Look through the eyepiece and focus the letter "e." Begin with the coarse adjustment and then bring the "e" into sharp focus with the fine adjustment. Is the "e" still right side up?

5. Now practice moving the "e" while you view it through the eyepiece. When the stage is moved to the right, which direction does the "e" move?

6. Practice moving the "e" up and down and right to left, demonstrating *translational movement* of the image.

7. View the "e" under 100× magnification.

PART III EXAMINATION OF NAILS

In this exercise you will examine the visible signs of the manufacturing process that produces nails. The automated machinery used to produce these nails leaves marks on the nails surface. Forensic investigators use these marks to match a manufactured product with a production plant or machine, or to the batch in which it was made. The marks that all the nails made by a particular method have in common are called **class characteristics.**

SAFETY

MATERIALS

5 - ¾-inch weather stripping (or similar) nails
Modeling clay, about the size of a quarter

PROCEDURE

1. Divide the clay into five sections and roll each into a ball.

2. Position the nail so the head is pointing toward you. Look for any machining marks present on the head of the nail.

3. View the nail under the microscope.

4. Examine each nail in the same manner. Be sure to point out the differences you observe. For example, are all five nails exactly the same shape? Is each head the same thickness as the others? Are they all the same length? These are examples of class characteristics. Do the striations appear to be identical? Is there a particular shape or mark that occurs on each nail that has no bearing on the quality or performance of the product?

EXERCISE 3 – THE VIRTUAL MICROSCOPE

Visit the "Virtual Microscope" web site to practice these techniques outside the laboratory:
http://micro.magnet.fsu.edu/primer/virtual/virtual.html
    Scroll down the page to find each of the following links.

Magnifying Microscopy

Visit the Magnifying Microscopy web link to practice selecting the best objective for the item you are viewing. Notice that as you increase the magnification, the portion of the object you are examining decreases. This is described as the field of view, and is an unchangeable restriction on the compound microscope.

Stereoscopic Zoom Microscopy

Using this simulation, you can change the **lamp intensity** (the amount of light streaming onto your sample), **zoom** control (how much the object is magnified), and **focus** (the crispness of the image as viewed through the eyepiece) of the image by moving the slider bars of each control feature. There are ten different samples to choose from, each requiring you to adjust the aforementioned settings before producing a clear image. Be sure to practice with the lamp intensity and take note of how an image can be made unclear by overilluminating or underilluminating the field of view.

Translational Microscopy

Visit the Translational Microscopy web link to practice focusing your image, changing magnification power and light source intensity, understanding the **translational movement** of the object when viewed through the eyepiece, and ultimately producing the best, most detailed image of the object you are examining. First select an item to view. Next, use the sliding bars to adjust the light intensity, focus, and magnification in the same manner as above.

Depth of Focus in Thick Samples

Visit this web link to view the phenomenon of focusing on the near, middle, or far aspects of a thick object like an insect or a group of fibers. First, select the object you wish to examine. Next, adjust the focus using the slider bar as you view the object to examine through its full thickness.

EXERCISE 4 – THE VIRTUAL COMPARISON MICROSCOPE

The comparison microscope allows the examiner to view two objects simultaneously. Each object is placed on its own stage, one to the left and one to the right. Each stage is like the ones on any other microscope with a stage micrometer and focus control. The examiner must orient each item at an angle useful for comparison.

These objects, like two bullets or cartridge casings, can be viewed one at a time, split-field, or superimposed. **Split-field** is most dramatic when viewing two bullets fired from the same gun. By shifting the bullets from left to right and back again, you can clearly line up the striae of matching bullets. The comparison microscope is also used in the forensic examination of hairs, fibers, and paint chips, to name a few.

This instrument is very expensive and your school is most likely not equipped with one. You can visit http://www.firearmsid. com to try your hand at using a comparison microscope. Through this web site you can experience the opportunity to operate this instrument just as a firearms examiner would.

First, **a brief explanation of how a bullet is fired** will help you understand how these items come to be marked in such a way as to be relevant to forensic investigation:

The **cartridge** is the casing, or shell, of a round that holds the **bullet**, gunpowder, and primer. When a gun is fired, the trigger releases a firing pin, which strikes the **breech face** of the cartridge. This ignites the primer, which lies directly in line with the pin. The primer ignites, setting off the gunpowder. The gunpowder produces an explosion, creating a sudden and powerful cloud of gas. The force of the expanding gas propels the bullet forward, directed through the barrel of the gun, and out toward its target. The impression of the firing pin is visible near the center, and the parallel scratches seen alongside are formed by the action of ejecting the empty cartridge. This produces unique markings on the breech face, which are used to relate a cartridge to the gun that fired it.

The barrels of most firearms are rifled, meaning there are small channels cut into the barrel in a spiral pattern. These grooves improve the accuracy of the gun by making the bullet rotate like a football as it travels through the air. The channels alter the bullet as it is forced through under high temperature and pressure, forming **lands and grooves** along the bullet's surface. The surfaces of the lands and grooves contain fine scratch or striation markings that are unique to each barrel. These striations enable a forensic ballistics examiner to match a bullet to the gun from which it was fired.

EXPLORE THE VIRTUAL COMPARISON MICROSCOPE

Your instructor has registered your class to give you access to the FirearmsID.com Virtual Microscope Lab. Enter the username and password provided by your instructor to test your skills with the **Cartridge Case ID**—Virtual Comparison Microscope (CCID-VCM). You can perform your own firearm cartridge comparison by selecting the Cartridge Case ID-VCM link. Read the instructions under the heading "What Is the CCID Virtual Comparison Microscope?" and then click *Test 1* from the upper right corner of the same page. Follow the instructions and see if you have the aptitude to be a firearms examiner!

The breech face of a cartridge is shown as it appears after the bullet it housed has been fired. Compare each unknown breech face impression to each of eight test samples shown on a split screen. Carefully focus and position the two breech faces so you can compare the scratches, gouges, or any other markings on each side by side. Click the key icon to the lower left of your screen to make a "match." Then select the next unknown and proceed in the same manner as before. Use the tally sheet to the right of the comparison window to track your progress. When you have completed all eight unknowns, click the diploma icon that appears at the lower right of the page to see your results. Proceed to *Test 2* through *Test 5*; each one is more challenging than the last.

Return to the main page and select the **Bullet ID**-VCM link. These tests are more challenging because you must compare all lands and grooves of each bullet to the same features on each test standard. The objects are already in focus, so you must adjust the position of each relative to the split screen. Click on "Get Final Result" to get your score.

Forensic Hair Analysis[8]

Hairs are persistent. Once transferred onto an object, like a blanket, a hair can travel great distances and remain intact spanning months, years, or even decades. Hairs are also quite tough. Like your fingernails, hairs are made of a protein called keratin. Hair is so strong, it has been found to exhibit greater tensile strength than a steel wire of the same gauge! For these reasons, hair is commonly discovered at a crime scene and preserved as evidence. Skill in the analysis of hair evidence is essential for a forensic scientist.

The most important instrument in the analysis of hair is the microscope. These exercises will serve to acquaint the student with the most widely used techniques in the forensic examination of hair.

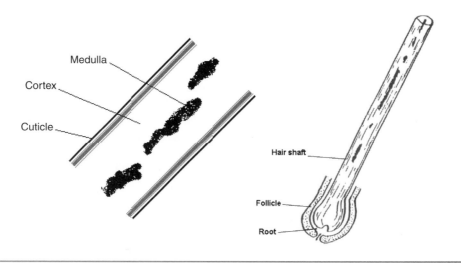

Figure 1   Basic morphology of hair.

---

[8] Please refer to the *Instructor's Manual* for additional preparation instructions relating to this experiment.

THE CUTICLE

This is the outer layer of the hair and it is comprised of overlapping scales pointing in the direction of hair growth. The major groups are an imbricate, coronal, or spinous cuticle.

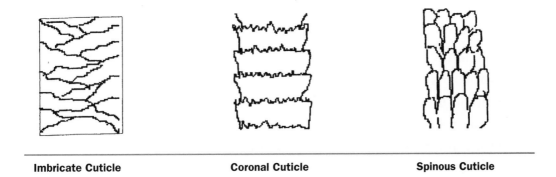

Imbricate Cuticle   **Coronal Cuticle**   **Spinous Cuticle**

THE MEDULLA

The medulla is the innermost portion of a hair, and its appearance varies between species and between human individuals. A hair can be scored based on the ratio of the width of its medulla to the width of the hair itself. This is called the **medullary index**. This is calculated by dividing the width of the medulla by the width of the hair shaft.

The medulla can be patterned or amorphous, as shown below. Patterned medullae are further designated as unisereal, multisereal, or lattice. Amorphous medullae are designated as fragmented, in which the medulla stops and starts along the length of the hair, or continuous.

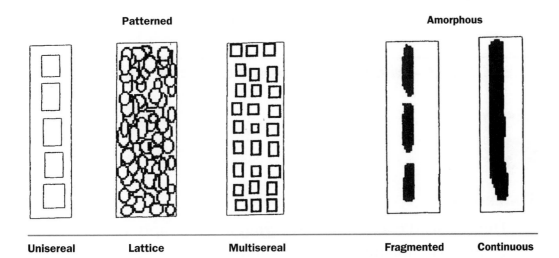

Patterned   Amorphous

Unisereal   **Lattice**   **Multisereal**   **Fragmented**   **Continuous**

EXERCISE 1 – CASTING SCALE PATTERNS

SAFETY

MATERIALS

Glass microscope slides
Isopropyl (rubbing) alcohol
Cotton balls
Clear nail polish
Human and nonhuman hair samples

PROCEDURE

1. Thoroughly clean the hair you intend to cast by pulling it through a tissue or cotton ball moistened with isopropyl alcohol.
2. Apply a very thin layer of clear nail polish to a glass slide in a long stripe.
3. Immediately lay the hair across the nail polish.
4. Allow the polish to dry and lift the hair out of the polish by the root end.
5. An imprint of the hair should be visible on the surface of the polish.
6. Place the slide on the microscope stage and begin viewing it under the lowest magnification.
7. Compare this to the actual hair—which is a better image for viewing the scale pattern?
8. Draw your findings into the table found in Exercise 2 and include comparisons to other animal hairs.

EXERCISE 2 – MICROSCOPIC IDENTIFICATION OF HAIR

SAFETY

MATERIALS

Human head hair samples, varying in color, and texture
Nonhuman (mammalian) hair samples

Ruler

Glass microscope slides, 75×50 are recommended

Glass coverslips

Glycerin or propylene glycol solution for cigar humidifiers
(available at tobacco shops and cigar retailers)

PROCEDURE

1. Place hair sample on a slide.
2. Apply a few drops of propylene glycol solution or glycerin
   to the slide.
3. Top with a coverslip.
4. Observe under 100× and 200× magnification.
5. Sketch the hair as indicated in the following table. Note
   the previously discussed morphological characteristics.
   Label these on your drawing.
6. Repeat the procedure for other samples. Compare the
   morphological differences between the human and nonhuman hairs with respect to medullary index, cuticle pattern, and medullary shape.

Sample Type	Sketch of Cuticle from Casts	Sketch of Medulla	Estimated Medullary Index
#1 Human			
#2			
#3			
#4			

EXERCISE 3 – COMPARISON OF HAIR EVIDENCE

SAFETY

MATERIALS

Evidence sample—head hair recovered from crime scene
Head hair exemplars provided by your instructor
Glass microscope slides, 75 × 50 are recommended
Glass coverslips
Glycerin or propylene glycol solution for cigar humidifiers
(available at tobacco shops and cigar retailers)

PROCEDURE

1. Place your evidential hair on the curl template on page 56 and assign a value from (00) to (09) for degree of curvature. If your hair exhibits more than one degree of curl, record the highest number. Enter this value into the following table.
2. Measure the length in centimeters and enter it into the following table.
3. Place the evidence hair sample on a slide.
4. Apply a drop of propylene glycol solution or glycerin.
5. Top with a coverslip.
6. Observe under 200× magnification.
7. Draw the hair to the best degree of detail possible.
8. Note physical and morphological characteristics as previously discussed. Label these on your drawing.
9. Repeat the procedure for exemplars.
10. Can you make an assertion as to a common origin between any of these hair samples?
11. Outline your findings in your laboratory notebook, using specific attributes to prove your hypothesis.

Sample Number	Approximate Length	Color	Degree of Curl	Type of Medulla
#1				
#2				
#3				
#4				
#5				
#6				

Diameter of Arc Circle (cm)

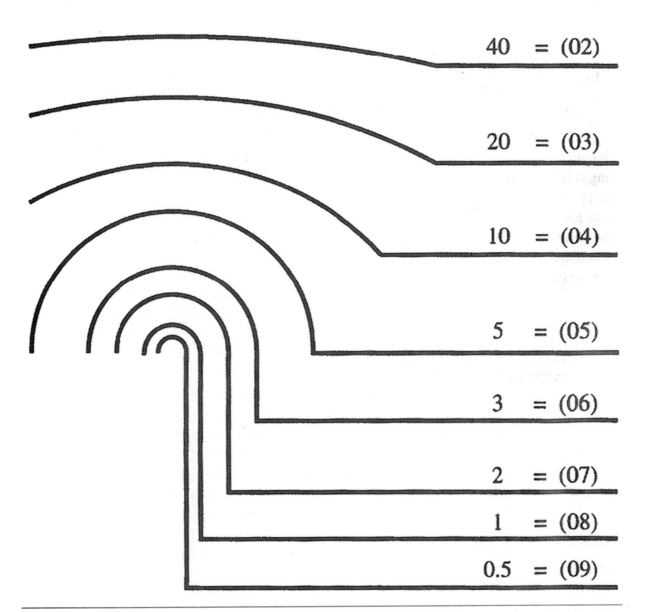

More Than   80   = (00)

Less Than:

80   = (01)

40   = (02)

20   = (03)

10   = (04)

5   = (05)

3   = (06)

2   = (07)

1   = (08)

0.5   = (09)

Handwriting Comparison[9]

CASE HISTORY

Hitler's Diaries

In 1981 a spectacular manuscript attributed to Adolf Hitler was disclosed by the brother of an East German general. These documents included Hitler's twenty-seven-volume diary and an unknown third volume of his autobiography, *Mein Kampf*. The existence of these works was both culturally and politically significant to the millions who were affected by World War II.

Authentication was undertaken by two world-renowned experts, one Swiss and one American. Both declared the handwritten manuscripts were identical to the known samples of Adolf Hitler's handwriting that they were given. Bidding wars began for publishing rights, and a major national U.S. newspaper won with a price near $4 million.

The publishing company that originally released the documents to the world market undertook its own investigation, which ultimately revealed a horrifying plot. The paper on which the diaries were written contained a whitener that didn't exist until 1954, long after Hitler committed suicide. The manuscript binding threads contained viscose and polyester, neither of which were available until after World War II. Further, the inks used in the manuscript were all inconsistent with those in use during the year these pages were allegedly written. Moreover, it was discovered that the exemplars sent to the Swiss and American experts as purportedly known examples of Hitler's handwriting were actually from the same source as the diaries. The experts were justified in proclaiming the documents were authentic because they *were* written

---

[9] Please refer to the *Instructor's Manual* for additional preparation instructions relating to this experiment.

by the same hand. However, chemical analysis of the inks later determined that the *Hitler Diaries* were in fact less than 1 year old—spectacular, but fake!

INTRODUCTION

Forged signatures are not the sole domain of students and their detention slips. Criminals of all ages attempt to defraud others by forging signatures, changing the dollar amount on a check, or even generating entire documents.

Documents may be forged in as many ways as they may be lawfully created, but these exercises will focus on the comparison of handwritten documents only. Among these are ransom notes, forged signatures, falsified checks, or a bogus last will and testament.

There are numerous features that document examiners look for when examining and comparing handwriting. The following are common aspects of variation in handwriting.

a. The slant of the lines—to the right or left, or no slant at all
b. The size of the letters relative to one another, capitalization and width versus height of each letter
c. Connecting strokes—between capitals and lowercase or among lowercase letters
d. Unique style gestures like curls or flourishes at the end of a letter or word
e. Adherence to the line—writing above, below, exactly on a line, or any deviation from beginning to end (starting on the line and trailing off below or above)
f. Crossing your "t's" and dotting your "i's"—presence or absence of these diacritics as well as their size, shape, and placement relative to the rest of the letter and word

---

EXERCISE 1 – A FAMOUS FORGERY!

In 1970, a man named Clifford Irving claimed to have made an agreement with the late Howard R. Hughes, aviation tycoon and film producer, and the McGraw-Hill Publishing Company to author Hughes's biography. To prove his claim, Irving produced signed letters addressed to himself from Hughes.

Forensic handwriting examiners were asked to determine the authenticity of the documents. Compare the following examples using the previously listed features and test your skills against theirs!

Example 1   Pictured in the following figure are actual case materials from the famous 1970 last will and testament forgery of aviation tycoon Howard Hughes.[10]

The letters on the left are from the forgery. Examples of Howard Hughes's known handwriting are on the right. Point out the differences between the two using specific examples.

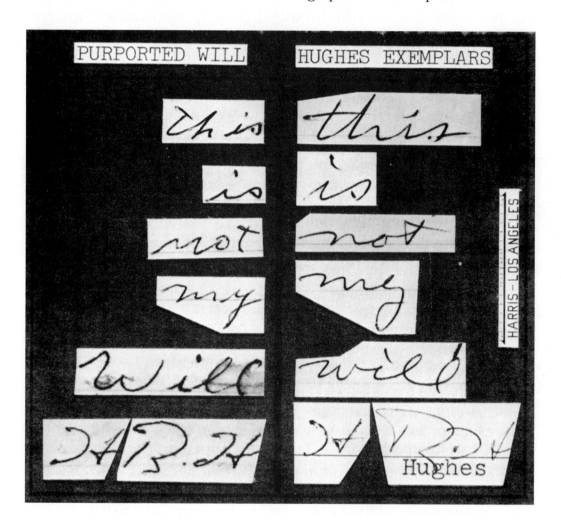

Notes:

_____

_____

_____

_____

_____

---

[10] Reprinted by permission of the American Society for Testing and Materials from the *Journal of Forensic Sciences,* copyright 1986.

Example 2   Shown in the following figure are examples of Howard Hughes's known signatures.[11] Are they identical to one another?

Howard R. Hughes
Standards

Exhibit B

1

2

3

4

5

6

Notes:

_____

_____

_____

_____

_____

[11] Reprinted by permission of the American Society for Testing and Materials from the *Journal of Forensic Sciences,* copyright 1975.

Example 3 Now compare the known signatures from Howard Hughes (from the previous figure) to the questioned signatures that follow. Even though Howard Hughes never signed his name the same way twice, a forger would not be able to disguise his own writing style. Point out similarities and differences between the known and questioned signatures. Attention should be paid to the letters "o" and "w" in Howard; "g", "h", and "es" in Hughes.

Notes:

_____

_____

_____

_____

_____

Is Your Signature the Same Every Time?

EXERCISE 2 – Are You a Good Forger?

1. Sign your name on the line below as you normally would.

   _____

2. Now, attempt to copy it *exactly,* three times.

   _____

   _____

   _____

Can you copy it perfectly? What differences do you notice between the first and subsequent attempts?

3. Describe these differences in the space provided below:

   _____

   _____

   _____

EXERCISE 3 – Disguising Your Handwriting

MATERIALS

Blue ball-point pen
Copy paper (unlined), 1 sheet per student
Desk lamp

Part I

1. Transcribe the exemplar statements on the paper provided by your instructor.

   Exemplar Statements

   a. Mary had a little lamb. His fleece was white as snow. Everywhere that Mary went, the lamb was sure to go.
   b. Hey diddle, diddle, the cat and the fiddle. The cow jumped over the moon. The little dog laughed to see such sport, and the dish ran away with the spoon.
   c. Row, row, row your boat gently down the stream. Merrily, merrily, merrily, merrily; life is but a dream!

2. Each statement should be written on a separate sheet of paper using only blue ball-point pen (no gel inks, markers, or fountain pens).

3. Write statements 1, 2, and 3 normally.

4. Write the statement at the top of each page. When you are finished, print your name on the back of each sheet toward the bottom.

5. Turn in all three pages of exemplars to your instructor.

Instructor: Assign a number to each student, and write it next to each exemplar text. Cut the signatures off the bottom. Use statement 3 as the questioned document, and pair it with statements 1 and 2 from the same and from other students. Distribute packets in the next lab period. Be sure students do not receive any of their own statements. The instructor decides if each packet will include the author of the questioned document!

Part II

1. Your instructor will provide several exemplars and a questioned document.

2. Your classmates will be given a different set of documents, so working together will not help—you are on your own this time!

3. You should not be reading for content, though any misspelling is important to note.

4. Look for how the author forms his or her letters *as the sum of its shapes*. It is the repeated occurrence of these shapes that define a writer's personal style, and make it recognizable as uniquely his or hers. These are unintentional, unconscious actions, and are extremely difficult to hide.

5. Record your findings in your notebook. Avoid making marks directly on any of the documents as this may confound future examination. If necessary, make a photocopy that you can use to illustrate your analysis.

6. The next step is to inspect the exemplars for similar characteristics. In each exemplar, look for the same letters you identified in your analysis of the questioned document.

7. Are you able to identify a suspect among the authors you investigated?

Paper Chromatography of Ink

The first step to analyzing the chemical constituents of a sample is to separate them. **Chromatography**, from the Greek for "color writing," has been expounded to suit the varying applications needed in forensic science. The basis of the technique depends on a chemical's unique **solubility** in a solvent, and its predictable and reproducible behavior when exposed to a solvent flow.

In chromatography, there is always a stationary phase and a mobile phase. The **stationary phase** is like the coffee you put in the basket of your drip coffee maker. The **mobile phase** is the hot water that flows over it, causing water-soluble chemicals to leave the ground beans and enter the water. This process is known as **extraction**. Chemicals that are **insoluble** in hot water will remain in the solid coffee grounds in the basket. This is an example which serves to acquaint you with the general concept—though it should be noted that brewing coffee is not an accepted chromatographic method!

Chromatography is a primary means of separating drugs out of biological samples for **identification** and **quantitation**. It is also used to develop a profile of chemical constituents in a substance to enable a comparison to a questioned item, like the pigments in a lipstick smudge found at a crime scene or the dyes from pen ink used to forge a signature.

Paper chromatography is an easy, inexpensive method of separating the constituents of a simple mixture. The sample is spotted on paper, allowed to dry, and then a solvent is allowed to creep up the paper by **capillary action**. As the solvent moves up the paper, it carries with it some of the constituents present in the sample spotted on the paper. A race ensues between these chemical constituents. Some will move faster than others, and hence a separation will take place.

SAFETY

CHROMATOGRAPHY OF BALL-POINT PEN INK

MATERIALS

Several blue ball-point pen samples: "exemplars"

Questioned document, written in blue ball-point ink

12-well ceramic spot plate

Pencil

1.5 × 3.5-inch strips of chromatography paper

Metric ruler

100 percent methanol

Dropper or Pasteur pipette with bulb

TLC development chamber, like a Coplin Jar—Alternately, you may use any small glass vessel with a lid

Wooden toothpicks, natural color

Scissors

Capillary tubes, at least one per sample

PROCEDURE

1. Add 5 to 8 mm 100 percent methanol to the chamber. This volume is designated in height because the size of the chamber you use will vary. Saturate the tank with methanol vapor by adding a piece of blotter paper to the chamber. Apply the lid and be sure the paper is thoroughly saturated by tilting or agitating the chamber a few times. Allow the chamber to equilibrate for at least 15 minutes.

2. Clip a 0.5-cm square from the text of each document and transfer each to a well of the spot plate. Be careful to keep track of your samples! You may want to draw a diagram in your notebook.

3. Add two drops methanol to each well.

4. Swirl plate *gently* or stir with a toothpick. You should observe the solvent turning blue or purple, showing that the ink is dissolving into the liquid.

5. Mark a pencil line 10-mm from the bottom of a short edge of the paper strip.

6. Make another line about ¾ of the way up the paper.

7. Measure the distance between the two lines in millimeters (mm) and record it in your notebook.

8. With your scissors, clip a triangular-shaped notch out of each side of the paper about 1 centimeter above the first line. These triangles should leave approximately 1 centimeter of intact paper between them.

9. Allow the extraction solvent to evaporate until the volume is reduced by 50 percent.

10. Using a capillary tube, draw up less than 0.5 cm of ink extract.

11. Apply a spot of each extract along the first pencil line. More is not necessarily better—do not apply too much! You may flank the sample from the questioned document by empty lanes to keep it separate from the exemplars. Be sure to use a clean capillary tube for each extract and to note the location of each sample in your notebook.

12. Allow samples to dry thoroughly.

13. Verify that 5-mm mobile phase is in the development chamber. Add more if necessary. Note: Be sure the depth of the mobile phase on the paper is BELOW THE SAMPLES once the paper strip is in place!

14. Position paper in the chamber, being careful not to disturb the solvent or splash any up onto the samples. Do not allow the paper to touch any edge or cling to a side of the chamber! This will produce distorted, unusable results.

15. Cover the chamber and wait until the solvent front has traveled *exactly* to your second pencil mark.

16. Remove the paper from the chamber and *allow it to dry completely*.

CALCULATING THE R_f VALUE

17. Mark the center of each band of sample 1. Measure the distance traveled by each band from the first pencil line (the starting line).

18. Record this distance in your notebook (mm). Do this for each sample. Is each ink separated into the same number of constituents? Are they all the same colors?

19. Now calculate the R_f value for each band by dividing the distance traveled by the band by the distance traveled by the solvent (i.e., the distance between the two pencil lines).

20. Each pen ink should yield a unique profile by compiling the number of bands and their corresponding R_f values, and their color. Be sure to include this information in your report.

21. Staple or tape your chromatograms to your notebook.

Thin-Layer Chromatography of Ink

Thin-layer chromatography (TLC) is used in this exercise because it is inexpensive, simple to perform, and one of the most common chromatographic methods in the forensic laboratory. This method's stationary phase is a thin layer of gel adsorbent coated onto plastic backing, called a TLC plate. As the liquid mobile phase is drawn into the gel, it is carried by **capillary action** up toward the top of the plate. Along the way, the samples are separated into their constituent chemicals.

SAFETY

MATERIALS

Pencil

Metric ruler

Precoated silica chromatography plate, 2.5×7.5 cm

Several blue ball-point pens, sampled on white paper (i.e., your "exemplars")

Questioned document, written in blue ball-point ink

95 percent ethanol, in a dropper bottle

Ethyl acetate

Distilled water

100-mL storage bottle with screw cap

12-well ceramic spot plate

Capillary tubes, at least one per sample

Developing chamber large enough to accommodate your TLC plate, like a Coplin Jar, or any solvent-safe container with a lid

REAGENT PREPARATION

To prepare the mobile phase:
Using a 25-mL graduated cylinder, add:

7.5 mL ethyl acetate

3.5 mL 95 percent ethanol

3.0 mL distilled water

to a 100-mL screw cap reagent storage bottle. Affix the cap tightly and invert three times to mix. Store at room temperature.

PROCEDURE

1. Add mobile phase to the chamber to attain a height of 5 millimeters. This is measured in millimeters because TLC chambers vary in size. It is important to note that *the level of the mobile phase should be below the level of the samples spotted on the plate!*

2. Saturate the tank with mobile phase vapors by adding a piece of blotter or filter paper to the chamber. Apply the lid and stand at least 15 minutes.

3. Examine the questioned (forged) document—do any of the exemplars resemble it either in color of ink or handwriting? Make a note of your preliminary observations.

4. Clip a 0.5-cm square from the text of each document and transfer each to a well of the spot plate. Be careful to keep track of your samples—make a list or diagram in your notebook.

5. Add two drops 95 percent EtOH to each well and **gently** swirl spot plate to agitate. You should observe the solvent turning blue or purple, indicating that the ink is dissolving into the liquid.

6. Mark a pencil line 10 mm from the bottom of a short edge of the TLC plate. Make another line about ¾ of the way up the plate.

7. Measure the distance between the two lines in millimeters (mm) and record it in your notebook.

8. Allow the solvent to evaporate until the volume is reduced by 50 percent. This should take about 5 minutes depending on ventilation and humidity. If your samples dry completely, reconstitute with a small drop of 95 percent EtOH.

9. Use a clean capillary tube for each sample to spot along the first pencil line. The spot should be no larger than twice the size of the period at the end of this sentence.

10. Be sure to note the location of each sample in your notebook. It may be helpful to draw a diagram.

11. Carefully and quickly position the TLC plate in the chamber and cover. You do not want to leave the chamber uncovered for more than a few seconds. Do not allow the silica side of the plate to touch any edge of the chamber and do not splash the mobile phase up onto the plate.

12. Check the progress of the solvent front every 2–3 minutes.

13. Stand until the solvent front has traveled *exactly* to your second pencil mark.

14. Remove the plate from the chamber and allow it to dry completely.

15. Draw a diagram of the plate, including each band (spot). You may want to photograph the plate to include in your report.

16. Mark the center of each band in the first sample. Measure the distance traveled by each band from the first pencil line. Record this distance in your notebook (mm). Repeat this process for each sample.

17. Calculate the R_f value for each band by dividing the distance traveled by the band by the distance between the two pencil lines (i.e., the distance traveled by the solvent).

18. Each ink should yield a unique profile by comparing the number of bands and their corresponding R_f values. Did any of the samples yield the same or similar profile? Do any of the exemplars compare to the questioned document?

19. Be sure to include this information in your report, along with the diagrams/photos of your TLC plate.

Blood Spatter Evidence

CASE HISTORY

Stephen Scher

A man banged on the door of a cabin in the woods outside Montrose, Pennsylvania. His friend, Marty Dillon, had just shot himself while chasing after a porcupine. The two had been skeet shooting at Scher's cabin, enjoying a friendly sporting weekend, when Dillon spotted a porcupine and took off out of sight. Dillon's friend, named Stephen Scher, heard a single shot and waited to hear his friend's voice. After a few moments, he chased after Dillon and found him lying on the ground near a tree stump, bleeding from a wound in his chest. Scher administered CPR after locating his dying friend, but he was unable to save Dillon who later died from his injuries. Police found that Dillon's untied boot had been the cause of his shotgun wound. They determined he had tripped while running with his loaded gun and shot himself. The grief-stricken Scher aroused no suspicion, so the shooting was ruled an accident.

Shortly thereafter, Scher moved from the area, divorced his wife, and married Dillon's widow. This was too suspicious to be ignored.

The crime scene was reconstructed to show that Scher's boots bore the unmistakable spray of high-velocity impact blood spatter, which is evidence that Scher was standing within an arm's length of Dillon when he was shot. This pattern of blood stains cannot be created while administering CPR, as Scher claimed. This also clearly refutes his claim that he did not witness the incident. In addition, the tree stump near the body bore the same type of blood spatter, in a pattern that indicates Dillon was *seated on the stump* and not running when he was shot. Finally, Dillon's ears were free of the high-velocity blood spatter that covered his face, but blood was on his hearing protectors found nearby. This is a clear indication that he was wearing his hearing protectors when he was shot and they were removed before investigators arrived. This and other evidence resulted in Scher's conviction for the murder of his long-time friend, Marty Dillon.

BLOOD PATTERN ANALYSIS

SAFETY

SUPPLIES

Commercially available simulated blood (available in movie or theatrical supply stores—Star Light & Magic http://www.starmgc.com/blood.html or Reel Creations http://www.reelcreations.com/store/store/) or prepare your own.
The following recipes have been proposed:[12]

1. Mix 4 oz. evaporated milk, 2 to 3 tablespoons tomato paste, and red food coloring. Add water as needed to achieve the approximate consistency of blood. Store in refrigerator for up to 2 days.
2. Mix dry milk powder, water, and red food coloring to desired thickness. Store in refrigerator.
3. Mix white corn syrup and red food coloring. Add water to desired thickness. Store at room temperature.

Disposable plastic pipettes
Protractor
Measuring tape
Smooth cardboard
Blotter paper
Roll of white paper, 36" wide, cut into 6-foot lengths
Digital or film camera

---

[12] T. Kubic and N. Petraco. *Forensic Science Laboratory Manual and Workbook, Revised Ed.* (Boca Raton, FL.: CRC Press, 2005).

PROCEDURE

Part I Cast-Off Spatter

1. In a designated area, place a 6-foot by 3-foot piece of paper on the floor.
2. Stand to the side of the paper, and, using a disposable pipette filled with simulated blood, walk along swinging your arm by your side in a natural motion.
3. "Blood" should stream from the pipette as you walk, landing on the paper. Do not flick or fling the "blood," as this will not produce usable results!! This is meant to simulate the "cast-off" spatter created when one walks carrying a bloody item.
4. Record the approximate height of the pipette from the floor (this will vary with the height and arm length of the individual).
5. Allow your paper to dry.
6. Photograph the individual spots in detail. Be sure to include scale and an arrow indicating the drop's orientation to the direction of travel (i.e., which way was the person walking).

Part II Impact Angle

1. Prop a smooth piece of cardboard (or other rigid surface) on a stack of books until the angle formed with the floor is 20°.
2. Dispense a single drop of simulated blood from a height of 24 inches. Avoid air bubbles in your dropper as they will deform the drop before it lands. If you need to try again, make sure your next drop is at least 3 inches away from the first!
3. Carefully remove the paper (do not disturb the shape of your drop!) to your bench and photograph it with scale.
4. Repeat procedure at 48 inches.
5. Change incident angle to 65° and repeat above at 24 and 48 inches.
6. Change incident angle to 90° and repeat above at 24 and 48 inches.
7. Repeat above procedure on blotter paper. This illustrates the effect that substrates of various textures have on the shape of a blood drop.

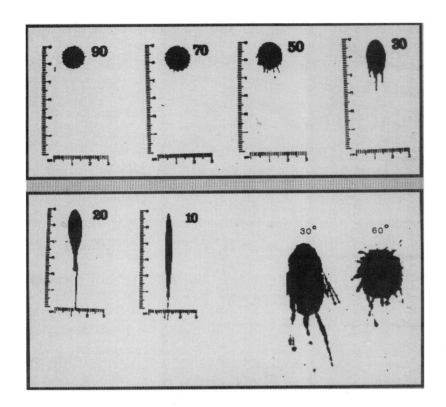

The first six stains were produced when blood drops landed onto smooth cardboard targets at the angles described. The last two stains were produced when blood drops landed onto irregular blotter paper at the angles described. *Courtesy Judith Bunker, J.L. Bunker & Associates, Ocoee, FL.*

Part III Calculations

Stain Shape vs. Impact Angle   Elongated stains have a distorted or disrupted edge that easily describes the direction of travel of the blood drop. The location or origin of bloodshed may be established by determining the directionality of the stain and the angle that blood impacted with the landing surface. The angle of impact is readily determined by a stain's length to width ratio and by applying the formula:

$$\text{Sin } A = \frac{\text{Width of bloodstain}}{\text{Length of bloodstain}}$$

where A = the angle of impact.

Example The width of a stain is 11 mm and the length is 22 mm.

Then, $\text{Sin } A = \dfrac{11 \text{ mm}}{22 \text{ mm}} = (11 \text{ mm} \div 22 \text{ mm}) = 0.50$

A scientific calculator having the trigonometric function will calculate that a sine of 0.50 is equal to a 30° angle.

Note: *There is a 5-degree error factor with this formula. This means that your calculations are good to plus or minus 5 degrees of the actual value of the angle of impact.*

STAIN SHAPE VS. IMPACT ANGLE

Measure the stain length and width in millimeters of the nine bloodstains shown on page 77. Use the previously described formula to calculate the angle of impact for each bloodstain. Record your findings in the following table.

Stain Number	Width	Length	Sine	Estimated Impact Angle
1	_____	_____	_____	_____
2	_____	_____	_____	_____
3	_____	_____	_____	_____
4	_____	_____	_____	_____
5	_____	_____	_____	_____
6	_____	_____	_____	_____
7	_____	_____	_____	_____
8	_____	_____	_____	_____
9	_____	_____	_____	_____

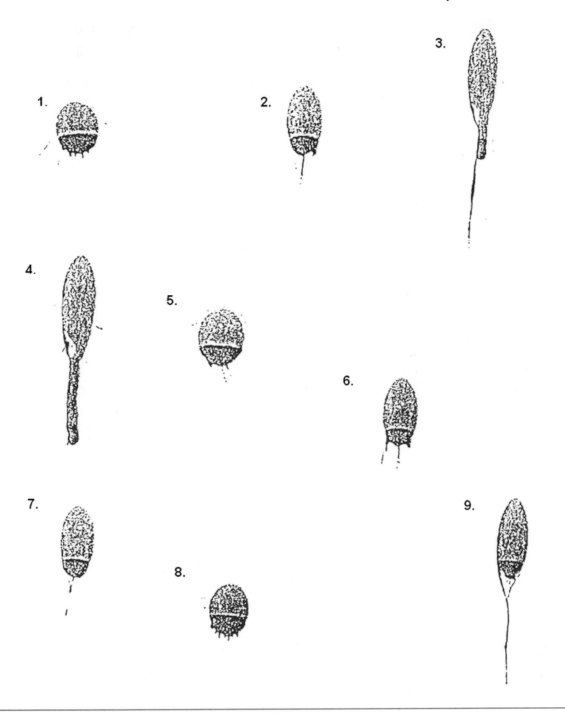

Courtesy Judith Bunker, J.L. Bunker & Associates, Ocoee, Florido.

PART IV EXAMINING YOUR WORK FROM PART II

1. Develop a numbering system to catalog your "blood spatter evidence" and assign a unique identifier to each "blood drop" and/or each photograph. Refer to your evidence in your report using its unique identifier.

2. Using the formula described in the previous section, calculate the angle of impact of the blood spatter patterns you created in Part II.

3. Do your calculations match the angles you used in your experiment?

4. Show your work in the space below:

Bloodstain Analysis[13]

A forensic scientist must enter an investigation without the luxury of a script or storyline. The crime scene is very rarely simple, and each should be approached with an objective and unprejudiced attitude. The forensic analysis of bloodstains abides by this same standard: before any bloodstain is sent to the laboratory for DNA or serology analysis, it must be determined to be blood! There are numerous substances that may appear to be blood. A presumptive test for the presence of blood spares the laboratory examiner the wasted time and effort of analyzing spattered motor oil, paint, or even common food items like barbecue sauce.

Even if the presumptive test confirms the presence of blood, the type of investigation depends heavily on the origin of the blood. Testing done within the laboratory can determine if blood evidence is from a human or animal source, which will aid police in mounting an investigation. Finally, human blood samples are tested using their DNA to positively identify the individual whose blood was recovered at the scene. Before DNA testing existed, blood typing analysis was used to narrow the field of possible suspects and victims. In this experiment, you will practice using presumptive tests, human/nonhuman antigen testing, and A-B-O blood group typing to identify an unknown sample.

The determination of blood is best made by means of a preliminary color test. The most common test used for this purpose is the chemical phenolphthalein. This test is also known as the *Kastle-Meyer color test*. The Kastle-Meyer color test is

---

[13] Please refer to the *Instructor's Manual* for additional preparation instructions relating to this experiment.

based on the observation that blood **hemoglobin** possesses peroxidase-like activity. Peroxidases are enzymes that accelerate the oxidation of several classes of organic compounds by peroxides. When a bloodstain, phenolphthalein reagent, and hydrogen peroxide are mixed together, the blood's hemoglobin will cause the formation of a deep pink color. Field investigators have found Hemastix® strips to be a useful presumptive field test for blood. Like the Kastle-Meyer test, Hemastix® strips will react with peroxidases. Designed as a urine dipstick test for blood, the strip can be moistened with distilled water and placed in contact with a suspect bloodstain. The appearance of a green color is indicative of blood.

EXERCISE 1 – PRESUMPTIVE TESTING WITH KASTLE-MEYER REAGENT

SAFETY

MATERIALS

Chicken blood or liver homogenate (1:3, in sterile water)

Single-ended cotton swabs

A piece of Styrofoam, to use as a swab stand

Sterile water in a dropper bottle

Phenolphthalein solution in a dropper bottle (Premixed solution available from DOJE's Forensic Supplies, http://www.dojes.com, Catalog # 310)

Hydrogen peroxide solution (3 percent) in a dropper bottle

"Evidence"—stains on fabric or paper, provided by your instructor (substances like liver homogenate, ketchup, shoe polish, lipstick). Those stains not visible when dry should be circled in pencil.

Prepare Your Kastle-Meyer Reagent

a. To 200 mL distilled water, add 4 g phenolphthalein, 40 g potassium hydroxide, and 20 g zinc dust.

b. Boil the mixture until the pink coloration has almost completely disappeared. Cool to room temperature and aliquot.

c. Store at 4°C. Before use, dilute an aliquot of stock solution with an equal volume of ethyl alcohol.

Alternately, commercially prepared presumptive blood testing reagents and kits can be purchased from DOJE's Incorporated, P.O. Box 500, Ocoee, Florida 407-880-8149.

PROCEDURE

Note: *When applying a drop of any reagent to the cotton tip of a swab, NEVER TOUCH THE DROPPER TO THE SWAB! Physical contact between the swab and the dropper will cause contamination. This will contaminate the entire reagent when you reinsert the dropper into the bottle!*

Part I Testing Your Reagents

1. Place two swabs on your swab stand by poking the free end of the swab down into the foam block. Place them approximately 3 inches apart.
2. Apply one drop of liver homogenate to swab #1. This is your **positive control**.
3. Apply one drop sterile water to swab #2. This is your **negative control**.
4. Apply one drop hydrogen peroxide to each swab.
5. Apply one drop phenolphthalein solution to each swab.
6. Your positive control should turn pink. Any future analysis which displays this result is considered to be a positive presumptive identification of blood.
7. Your negative control should not show ANY change. Any future analysis that displays this result is considered to be a negative test for blood. If your negative control turns pink, even a little, alert your instructor and/or ask for new reagents and swabs.
8. Good practice dictates that a negative control should be included with every test batch.

Part II Testing Your "Evidence"

1. Label the "evidence" you have been assigned. Each item should receive a number.
2. Work with only one item at a time. Do not allow the items to touch one another. Also, *do not stand or lean over* a piece of evidence while you are working. Reagents can drip onto it and compromise your analysis!
3. Prepare two swabs by moistening the tip of each with one drop of sterile water.

4. Set one swab aside as your negative control.
5. Roll the other swab over the stain. If you have an item with a circle marked on it, you should swab the center of the circle.
6. Apply a drop of hydrogen peroxide to each swab. Do you see a color change?
7. Apply a drop of phenolphthalein to each swab. Do you see a color change?
8. Record your findings in your notebook.
9. Repeat this process for each piece of "evidence."

EXERCISE 2 – PRESUMPTIVE TESTING WITH HEMASTIX®

SAFETY

MATERIALS

Hemastix®, available from local pharmacy

Plain wood toothpicks (not dyed)

Sterile water in a dropper bottle

Chicken blood or liver homogenate (1:3, in sterile water)

"Evidence"—stains on fabric or paper, provided by your instructor (substances like liver homogenate, ketchup, shoe polish, lipstick). Those stains not visible when dry should be circled in pencil.

PROCEDURE

Part I Testing Your Reagents

1. Remove two Hemastix® test strips from the container without touching the spongy pad on the end. Place them on your bench with the pad facing up.
2. Apply one drop of sterile water to the pad of each strip. Note: The end of the dropper should *not* make contact with the test strip! The test pad should remain yellow in color.
3. Set aside one of the two strips. This is your **negative control**.
4. Your negative control should not show ANY change. Any future analysis that displays this result is considered to be a negative test for blood. (If your negative control turns

greenish, even a little, alert your instructor and/or ask for new supplies.)

5. Apply one drop liver homogenate to the second strip. This is your **positive control**.

6. The spongy pad on your positive control should turn green. Any future analysis which displays this result is considered to be a positive presumptive identification of blood. Remember, these test strips produce this same response to *any* sample containing peroxidase, for example, potato juice and horseradish, so a green color change is NOT definitive proof of the presence of blood!

7. Good practice dictates that a negative control should be included with every test batch.

Part II Testing Your "Evidence"

1. Label the "evidence" you have been assigned. Each item should receive a number.

2. Work with only one item at a time. Do not allow the items to touch one another.

3. Prepare two test strips by moistening the pad on each with one drop of sterile water.

4. Set one strip aside as your negative control.

5. Scratch the end of a clean toothpick over the stain. If you have an item with a circle marked on it, you should take a sample from the center of the circle.

6. Touch the tip of the toothpick to the pad of the second test strip. Do you see a color change?

7. Record your findings in your notebook.

8. Repeat this process for each piece of "evidence."

EXERCISE 3 – IMMUNOASSAY[14]

Immunoprecipitation assay, or **immunoassay**, is a technique widely used by forensic scientists for determining the species origin of biological materials. A number of techniques have been devised for performing immunoassay tests on bloodstains. One method, called *gel diffusion,* takes advantage of the fact that antibodies and antigens will diffuse or move toward one another on an agar gel-coated plate. Here, the extracted bloodstain and the human antiserum are placed in separate holes opposite each other

---

[14] Courtesy of Joanne Long, Faculty of Cherry Hill High School East, Cherry Hill, New Jersey, as adapted from *Shoestring Biotechnology,* copublished by the National Association of Biology Teachers and the Biotechnology Institute, 2002.

on the gel. If the blood is of human origin, a line of precipitation will form where the antigens and antibodies meet. Similarly, the antigens and antibodies can be induced to move toward one another under the influence of an electrical field. In the *electrophoretic method,* an electrical potential is applied to the gel medium; a specific antigen–antibody reaction will be denoted by a line of precipitation formed between the hole containing the blood extract and the hole containing the human antiserum.

CASE HISTORY

Police are called to the scene of a hit and run accident in a rural area. The scene is on a major highway, but the surrounding area is not densely populated. The surrounding county supports a large population of wildlife, including deer, raccoon, and skunk.

The victim was transferred to a local hospital and police conduct interviews with several witnesses. All witnesses recall the same make and model of car, a silver compact, and one witness provides a partial license plate. This leads police to a residence where they find the suspect vehicle with a damaged front bumper and cracked headlight. On the headlight there are reddish-brown marks that show a positive result with the Kastle-Meyer reagent, a presumptive test for blood.

The suspect tells the police that he did hit something, but not on the night of the hit and run. He says he recalls hitting a deer approximately 1 week earlier. Police remove the suspect's car to the lab, where a sample of the reddish-brown stain is entered into evidence.

Your job as the forensic scientist assigned to the case is to determine if the blood sample taken from the suspect's vehicle came from a human or from an animal.

SAFETY

MATERIALS

One agar plate (instructions below)
One soda straw

One set of simulated sera and antisera, provided by your instructor

Yellow colored water

Blue colored water

Preparation of 2 percent agar plates (makes two)

Water

Powdered agar

250-mL beaker

2 petri or tissue culture dishes

Hotplate or microwave oven

1. Boil 50 g of water in a wide-mouthed vessel. A microwave oven may be used.
2. Add 1 g of powdered agar to the water and stir until completely dissolved.
3. Pour approximately 20 mL of the liquid agar into a petri dish.
4. Stand at room temperature to solidify. Apply the lid and add your group name and date.

PROCEDURE

1. Turn your solidified agar plate upside down so that you are looking at the underside of the solid agar.
2. Position the plate over the reversed-image template shown in Figure 1. Label the plate *exactly* as the reversed-image template appears.
3. Turn the plate back over and remove the lid. The labels should now appear legible, as shown in Figure 2.
4. Using the labels drawn on the bottom as a guide, use the straw to remove plugs of agar from each of the areas labeled. Crimp the top of the soda straw by folding it over and pinching it between your fingers. Insert the open end into the gel and twist. Release the folded end of the straw and remove the straw from the gel. A plug of gel should stay inside the straw. Remove the plug by flicking the straw over the edge of a sink or trash can. Do not deform the end of the straw when removing the gel plug! Repeat at each labeled location on the plate.
5. Add drops of the following to each well as indicated. Add one drop at a time and **do not overfill** the well. Avoid cross-contamination by using ONLY the droppers in each container.

- Well Y—add yellow food coloring
- Well B—add blue food coloring
- Well HA—add simulated human antiserum
- Well HS—add simulated human serum
- Well DA—add simulated deer antiserum

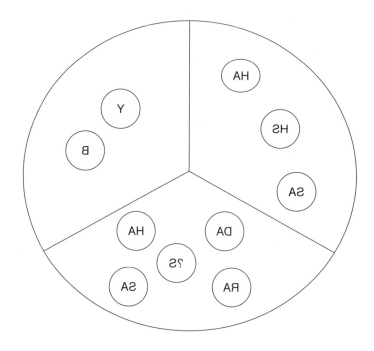

Figure 1   Reversed-image template.

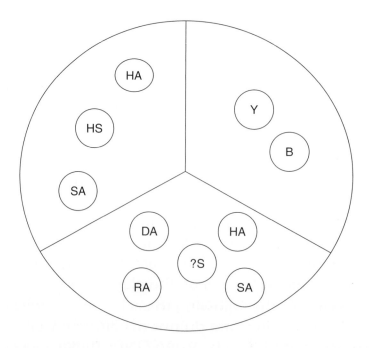

Figure 2   Finished appearance of your agar plate.

- Well RA—add simulated raccoon antiserum
- Well SA—add simulated skunk antiserum
- Well ?S—add simulated unknown serum from suspect's car

6. Make observations of your plate at 15-minute intervals for approximately 45 minutes.

7. Describe what occurs between the wells containing the yellow and blue food colorings.

8. What's the source of "?S"?

EXERCISE 4 – BLOOD TYPING

SAFETY

MATERIALS

Commercially available simulated blood typing kit (Carolina Biological Supply Company, Item # FR 70-0101)
Including:
  Synthetic blood
  Synthetic antisera
  "Questioned blood sample"
  Spot plate or blood typing slide
  Toothpicks or mixing sticks

PROCEDURE

1. Place a drop of a synthetic blood sample into each well of three wells of your spot plate.

2. To the first well, add a drop of anti-A synthetic serum.

3. To the second well, add a drop of anti-B synthetic serum.

4. To the third well, add a drop of anti-Rh synthetic serum.

5. Using a new toothpick for each well, mix for approximately 20 seconds.

6. Examine the first well. If the liquid is smooth, no agglutination has occurred. If lumps/solid particles appear in the liquid, agglutination has occurred. This means that the sample contains the antigen targeted by the antiserum. Therefore, it is positive or that blood type.

7. Repeat for each sample using a clean spot plate or slide.

Thin-Layer Chromatography of Liquid Lip Color

Thin-layer chromatography (TLC) is used in this exercise because it is inexpensive, simple to perform, and one of the most common chromatographic methods in the forensic laboratory. This method's stationary phase is a thin layer of silica adsorbent coated onto plastic backing, called a TLC plate. As the liquid mobile phase is drawn into the silica, it is carried by **capillary action** up toward the top of the plate. Along the way, the lipstick samples are separated into their constituent chemicals. Any constituent not soluble in the mobile phase, like solid flakes, will remain in the original location.

SAFETY

MATERIALS

Pencil

Metric ruler

Precoated thin layer chromatography plate

Three (3) Liquid Lip Color exemplars of similar color, portioned onto glass slides.

> *L'Oreal Liquid Lip, Black Radiance Liquid Lip Color, Maybelline Wetshine Liquid Lip Color, Max Factor Gel Lip Color* and *Revlon Lip Glide* products are recommended for use with this experiment.

Sample of the lip color found at the crime scene, on a glass slide

Ethyl acetate

95 percent ethanol

Distilled water

Dropper or Pasteur pipette with bulb

Capillary tubes, at least one per sample

Developing chamber (any solvent-safe container with a tight-fitting lid)

Iodine crystals (Sirchie Cat # A211C)

Fuming chamber—250-mL beaker with a large watchglass as a lid

Mug warmer or hotplate (Sirchie Cat # FHP100)

REAGENT PREPARATION

To prepare the mobile phase using a 10-mL graduated cylinder, add:

7.5 mL ethyl acetate

3.5 mL 95 percent ethanol

3.0 mL distilled water

to a 100-mL screw cap bottle. Affix the cap tightly and invert three times to mix. Store the mobile phase at room temperature.

PROCEDURE

1. Add 5–7 mm mobile phase to the chamber. This is measured in millimeters because TLC chambers vary in size. It is important to note that *the level of the mobile phase should be below the level of the samples spotted on the plate*!

2. Insert a piece of blotter or filter paper and moisten it with the mobile phase by leaning the chamber onto its side. Apply the lid. Allow the chamber to become saturated with mobile phase vapor for at least 15 minutes.

3. Handle the TLC plate carefully—hold it by the edges and/or corners only! Mark a pencil line 10 mm from the bottom of a short edge of the TLC plate. Make another line about ¾ of the way up the plate. Note: You are concerned with the white silica side and not the shiny plastic side of the plate.

4. Measure the distance between the two lines in millimeters (mm) and record it in your notebook.

5. Examine the samples provided by your instructor. Record their appearance in your notebook. Note the color, opacity, and the presence of any particulates present in the lip color like glitter or metallic flakes. Assign a number to each sample to use when referring to it in your report. Be sure to keep track of your samples!

6. Obtain a small beaker containing about 5 milliliters of ethyl acetate.

7. Use a capillary tube to draw up some of the ethyl acetate (extraction solvent). Do this by grasping the tube by the middle and touching it to the surface of the solvent. Capillary action will carry a small amount of the ethyl acetate up into the tube. This will only work if your capillary tube is open at both ends! Cover the top of the tube with your fingertip and move the tube over one of your lip color samples.

8. Remove your finger from the top of the tube. Grasp the tube by the middle and gently tap the tube directly onto one of your samples. Continue tapping until the solvent has been evacuated from the tube. Move the tube in a circular motion, as though you are stirring the solvent into the lip color. You should observe the solvent dissolving a small portion of the lip color.

9. Draw up approximately 0.5 cm high and spot three times (Allow the solvent to dry in between—you will see a bright ring around the sample start to disappear). The spot should be no more than twice the size of the period at the end of this sentence. Space the samples far enough apart so they can be distinguished from one another and do not run together. Four samples for a 2.5 cm-wide plate are recommended.

10. Repeat for each sample. *Use a clean capillary tube for each lip color.*

11. You may flank the sample from the "crime scene" with an empty lane or some extra space to keep it separate from the "exemplars."

12. Be sure to note the location of each sample in your notebook! It may be helpful to draw a diagram.

13. *Carefully* and quickly position the TLC plate in the chamber and cover. You do not want to leave the chamber uncovered for more than a few seconds. Do not allow the mobile phase to splash up onto the plate. Pay particular attention to the silica side of the plate. Do not allow it to rest on any surface inside the chamber because capillary

action will carry the mobile phase up the edges of the silica and produce a curved solvent front. This will yield a distorted, unusable result.

14. Check the progress of the solvent front every few minutes. Stand until the solvent front has traveled *exactly* to your second pencil mark.

15. Remove the plate from the chamber and avoid touching the silica. Allow it to dry completely.

16. Follow these instructions to treat your plate with iodine fumes. This treatment will enhance the appearance of some lipstick components, making them visible against the white silica plate.

    a. Inside the fume hood, arrange a mug warmer or hotplate under a 250-mL beaker. Add approximately two dozen iodine crystals to the beaker.

    b. Insert the TLC plate into the chamber and allow it to lean against the side of the beaker. Do not allow the iodine crystals to contact the TLC plate. Apply the lid (watchglass).

    c. Close the fume hood and turn on the hotplate to a low setting.

    d. Carefully monitor the development of the liquid lip color samples.

    e. Do not overdevelop! Applying too much iodine can permanently discolor the TLC plate.

17. Mark the center of each band in the first sample. Measure the distance traveled by each band from the first pencil line. Record this distance in your notebook (mm). Repeat this process for each sample. If your samples are streaky, record the distance from the first pencil line to the nearest point. It may be helpful for writing your report to draw a diagram or photograph your plate.

18. Calculate the R_f value for each band by dividing the distance traveled by the band by the distance between the two pencil lines (i.e., the distance traveled by the solvent).

19. Each lip color should yield a unique profile by comparing the number of bands and their corresponding R_f values. Did samples of the same color yield the same profile?

20. Be sure to include this information in your report, with the diagrams/photos of your TLC plate. Do any of the "exemplars" compare to your "crime scene" sample?

Tool Mark Analysis[15]

The shape, size, and pattern of a tool may be discernable by the markings the tool leaves on a softer object. This kind of determination falls under the heading of **class characteristics** because it is indistinguishable from other similarly manufactured tools and will not tell investigators which of the thousands of identical tools actually made the marks in question.

More often, the tool marks are compared to a tool recovered either at the scene or from a suspect. In this situation, investigators aim to determine whether or not *that specific tool* made the evidential marks. This is done by comparing the striations, defects, burrs, and any other features unique to the tool, as revealed during control laboratory tests, to the tool marks collected from the crime scene. These properties are called **individual characteristics** because they are unique to each tool.

During the normal use of a tool, like a flathead screwdriver, it accumulates wear marks and defects along the surface of the blade. These defects are unique to that tool and impart it with individual characteristics, meaning the likelihood of finding another flathead screwdriver of the same size bearing identical defects is so unlikely as to be considered impossible. When that screwdriver is used to pry open an aluminum screen door, the contact of the blade against the metal door will create scratches with a unique pattern of stripes, called striations.

EXERCISE 1 – COMPARISON OF TOOLS

MATERIALS

Four to six hand tools (e.g., pliers, screwdriver, or vise grips)
Hand lens

---

[15] Please refer to the *Instructor's Manual* for additional preparation instructions relating to this experiment.

PROCEDURE

1. Examine the working edges/surfaces of each tool. Look carefully at the sharp or working edges—are they worn? Have they been sharpened? Is this tool brand-new? Note any gouges, breaks, or irregular edge patterns.
2. Draw each edge as you see it under the magnifying hand lens (in the most detail you can).
3. Make a data table to organize your findings concerning state of wear, notable defects, or general age of tool.

EXERCISE 2 – CASTING TOOL MARKS

MATERIALS

Six hand tools per lab group
Modeling clay or silicone-based material
Scrap paper or a small paper plate
Wooden craft stick (Popsicle® stick or tongue depressor)
"Evidence"—a piece of wood or other soft material bearing a tool impression
Stereoscopic microscope
Metric ruler

PROCEDURE

1. Examine the tools on your lab bench one at a time.
2. In detail, describe the physical appearance, color, weight, and any lettering or brand seals apparent on the tool. Record the dimensions of the tool itself and its working edge(s). A reader should be able to visualize the tool from your description. If possible, photograph or sketch the tool to be included in your report.
3. Determine the most likely uses for and orientation of these tools in the production of the tool mark "evidence" assigned to you.
4. Examine the item labeled as "evidence" (given to you by your instructor) under the stereoscopic microscope.
5. Note any patterns, scratches, or defects apparent on the item. Is there a tool mark on this item?
6. If so, measure the evidential mark and record the dimensions in your notebook.
7. For purposes of instruction, clay may be used in place of a silicone casting material. It should be noted that a

silicone-based product is used at crime scenes. Apply a portion of clay or silicone over the tool impression with a craft stick or your fingers. Press the clay onto the object so as to fill the fine details of the impression.

8. Carefully peel back the cast without deforming the material by pulling or twisting it. A high-quality cast will increase your chances of success, so be gentle!

9. View the cast under the stereoscopic microscope.

10. Note any patterns, scratches, or defects apparent in the cast.

11. Use your ruler to measure its dimensions and record these in your notebook.

12. Sketch the cast, indicating its unique features.

13. Visually compare the "evidence" cast you made with the suspect tools (see Figure 1).

14. Remember that you may need to orient the cast in a way that may not immediately make sense to you to find a good comparison! Be sure to look for those unique patterns, scratches, or defects that you found on the tools.

15. Compare the dimensions of the evidential mark to the measurements from the suspect tools, as shown in Figure 1.

Figure 1   Comparison of the cast of a tool mark impression with a suspect tool. *Courtesy Sirchie Fingerprint Laboratories, Inc., Youngsville, North Carolina.*

16. This should enable you to identify the best candidate tool, or confirm that the tool which made the mark now in evidence is not represented in the field of items selected for analysis.

17. Prepare a report outlining your conclusions as to the tool that made the evidential mark. Include an assessment of your comfort level with this identification you have made, and demonstrate your conclusions relative to the possibility of a match, if applicable.

18. If you were not able to attribute the evidential mark to any of the suspect tools, establish your reasoning for this conclusion through a complete, detailed explanation of your findings.

19. Make recommendations to investigators and evidence collectors for improving their methods. Can you think of an item that an investigator could search for at the crime scene that would help you to complete your analysis?

EXERCISE 3 – EXAMINATION OF TOOL MARK CHARACTERISTICS

SAFETY

MATERIALS

Flathead screwdriver or a crowbar taken from "crime scene"
Ruler
Block of soft wood
Aluminum or copper tooling foil, 5 × 5" sheet
Hand lens

PROCEDURE

1. Examine the screwdriver on your lab bench. Measure the length of the blade and handle and record this in your notebook. Also, record any writing, brand logos, or unique marks visible on the surface of the tool.

2. Place the aluminum or copper sheet over the block of wood. Make a tool mark by pressing the flat side of the head of the screwdriver or crowbar onto the aluminum or copper, using both hands to press down into the metal. Make a deep mark. This should mimic the motion of prying open a window.

3. Make three more marks, varying the pressure you apply each time.

4. Turn the screwdriver or crowbar over and repeat the previous procedure on a new section of the aluminum or copper sheet.

5. Use your hand lens to examine the impressions. Pay attention to any features that reveal the dimension and shape of the tool. These features are not unique and are referred to as class characteristics. Look for any evidence of the unique marks you found on the surface of the tool in step 1. These features are called individual characteristics.

6. If provided by your instructor, compare your test impressions to a "window sill from the crime scene" bearing "pry marks." Could the screwdriver you examined be the tool used to gain entry into this crime scene? Explain which markings are examples of class characteristics and which are individual characteristics.

Footwear Impressions[16]

CASE HISTORY

The O.J. Simpson Trial—Who Left the Impressions at the Crime Scene?

On the night of June 12, 1994, Nicole Brown, ex-wife of football star O.J. Simpson, and her friend Ron Goldman were brutally murdered on the grounds outside her home in Brentwood, California. O.J. Simpson was arrested for their murders, but maintained his innocence. The bloody crime scene revealed bloody shoe impressions along the concrete walkway leading up to the front door of her condominium. These shoe impressions were of extremely high quality and of intricate detail. The news media broadcast countless images of these bloody shoeprints on television, making it obvious to the killer that those shoes would surely link him to the crime.

William J. Bodziak, the famed FBI shoeprint examiner, investigated the footwear evidence from the scene. His first undertaking was to identify the brand of shoe that made these marks. Since the pattern was very clear and distinct, with complete associated toe-to-heel detail, this seemed a simple task at first. Bodziak compared this pattern to the thousands of sole patterns in the FBI's database. None matched. He then went to his reference collection of books and trade show brochures with no success. His experience told him these were expensive, Italian-made casual dress shoes with a sole made from synthetic material. He shopped the high-end stores for a similar tread pattern, but he was still unable to identify the shoes. Then he drew a composite sketch of the sole and faxed the image to law enforcement agencies and

---

[16] Please refer to the *Instructor's Manual* for additional preparation instructions relating to this experiment.

shoe manufacturers and distributors worldwide. The owner of the American distributing company for Bruno Magli shoes was the only one to respond.

Further exhaustive investigation revealed these were extremely rare shoes. There were two styles of shoe bearing this exact sole design. They were available for only 2 years, and from a mere forty stores in the United States and Puerto Rico. The *Lorenzo* style shoe had a boot-like upper that came to the ankle. The *Lyon* style shoe had the lower, more typical dress shoe cut. Since the impressions were made by a size 12 shoe, it was later determined that only 299 pairs of size 12 with this tread pattern were sold in the United States. Simpson flatly denied ever owning these shoes, adding he would never wear anything so ugly. However, he was known to wear a size 12.

Photographs taken almost 9 months prior to the murders show Simpson wearing a pair of black leather Bruno Magli *Lorenzo* shoes. These shoes were available in several colors, so this narrows the number of shoes matching Simpson's pair of *Lorenzos* (this size, color, and style) sold in the United States to twenty-nine pairs.

Proving Simpson owned a pair of shoes that had the exact pattern found printed in blood at the crime scene was an essential component of the case, but it was not done in time to be used during the criminal prosecution. The photographs of Simpson in his Bruno Magli shoes were released after the culmination of the criminal trial, so the jury never heard the direct evidence that Simpson owned these shoes. This proved to be an important link uniting Simpson with the crime scene in the civil trial. O.J. Simpson was acquitted of the murders of Nicole Brown and Ron Goldman in the criminal trial, but found to be responsible for their murders in the civil court case.

INTRODUCTION

Shoeprints and impressions may be found at any type of crime scene, and can provide a primary means to identify or exclude a suspect. The distinction drawn between prints and impressions is an important one: prints are two-dimensional, while impressions are three-dimensional. Thus, the preferred methods of collection are quite different. In the first exercise, you will make an impression and collect it as evidence by casting it— that is, making a mold and preserving it for analysis in the lab just as if you were a crime scene technician. In the third exercise you will analyze the cast and compare it to a footwear sample.

EXERCISE 1 – MAKING A CAST

MATERIALS

A shoebox, large enough for your footwear
Soil
Ruler
One small can of inexpensive aerosol hair spray
Large mixing bowl (or 1-gallon zip-top bag)
Paint stirrer or large, long-handled spoon
Five-pound bag of Plaster of Paris (or dental stone)
Water
Wire hangers, clipped into 3- to 4-inch pieces, or craft sticks

PROCEDURE

1. Fill your shoebox half-way with dry soil. Tamp lightly and level the surface with your ruler.
2. Place your selected footwear onto the soil and push down to make an impression approximately $\frac{1}{2}$ inch deep.
3. Carefully lift the shoe out of the soil, trying not to knock any loosened pieces of soil into the impression.
4. Holding the can of hairspray about 8 inches from the soil, apply an even layer to the impression using a sweeping motion. Be sure that even the deepest edges of the impression receive the same amount of coverage. More is not necessarily better—do not overapply!
5. Allow to stand for 10 minutes to allow the hairspray to dry.
6. Add $\frac{1}{2}$ of the 5-pound bag of Plaster of Paris to a large mixing bowl.* Add enough water to the bowl to produce a pancake batter-like consistency. No lumps, please!! (Again, the amount of water you need will vary with the ambient humidity and plaster manufacturer.)
7. Pour the plaster into the impression, using a paint stirrer to broadcast the stream so it does not destroy the fine details of the impression. Pour to reach at least $\frac{1}{2}$ inch in thickness.
8. Place the cut-up hangers or craft sticks horizontally and vertically on the surface of the wet plaster. These will serve to reinforce the cast.
9. Prepare a second mix of Plaster of Paris in the same way and apply it over the first to a total thickness of at least 1 inch.

10. Label the wet plaster surface with the date and your name or group number before it dries.

11. Store it to dry completely overnight.

Alternately, you can measure the Plaster of Paris into a 1-gallon size plastic zip-top bag and add the water in increments. Seal the bag and mix by working back and forth with your fingers. Dental stone may be substituted for the Plaster of Paris. This material can be preweigh and mixed with a measured amount of water according to the manufacturer's instructions.

You can view the preparation of a footwear impression cast using dental stone on the web at www.sccja.org/csr-mix.htm. Dental stone is much harder than Plaster of Paris and does not require a second pouring and reinforcement.

EXERCISE 2 – FOOTWEAR COMPARISON[17]

Compare the paired images below. For each pair of footwear impressions, note individual characteristics. This means that you should look for a cut, gouge, tear, imbedded pebble, or pattern of wear which is unique to that shoe. Indicate this unique characteristic on each of the paired images.

Figure 1   Locate at least seven individual characteristics.

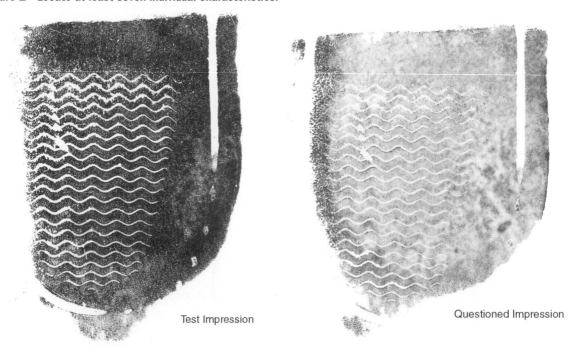

Test Impression

Questioned Impression

[17] Figures 1 and 2 courtesy of William J. Bodziak, Special Agent FBI, Retired, Palm Coast, Florida.

Figure 2 Locate at least four individual characteristics.

Electrostatic
Lift (reversed)

Known Shoe
Reverse Photograph

EXERCISE 3 – CAST/FOOTWEAR COMPARISON

PROCEDURE

1. Collect your cast prepared in Exercise I and rinse any loose soil from it under the tap. Do not scrub or pick off anything! Pat dry with paper towels. Place your cast and exemplar selection into the box. *Be sure to include the shoe you used to make the impression!*

2. Exchange boxes with another lab group.

3. Survey the "evidence" from your new box. Your group will have to devise a numbering scheme which assigns unique identifiers to each piece of evidence. *Make sure that you are able to refer to an item in your report without confusion.*

4. List each item in your notebook under its unique identifier and write a brief description. Include manufacturer, size (if indicated), color, and condition. Affix evidence tags bearing the evidence number, your initials, and today's date.

5. Organize your evidence on the bench: place the cast off to one side and the footwear exemplars to the other.

6. Measure the dimensions of the cast in centimeters and record this in your notebook. Do the same for each exemplar.

7. Position an adjustable light source over the cast to make the depth and details more apparent. Rotate the cast and examine all sides for unique features. Look for cuts that interrupt the pattern on the sole, wear or rub marks on the outer edge, or even apparent manufacturing defects.

8. Make a note of each feature and refer to each in your report. You may choose to identify each feature with a unique number or letter. If available, take a photograph of the cast to use in your report. On the photograph, indicate each feature using its identifier.

9. Next, examine each of the exemplars in the same manner.

10. By comparing length, width, sole pattern, and unique features, you should be able to deduce which exemplar is the most likely mold for the impression found at the "crime scene." Outline your findings in your report using explicit examples.

Forensic Entomology

The order of natural events following a death at an outdoor location begins with the appearance of any number of fly species. The arrival of insects, such as the blow fly, to a death scene is inevitable and almost immediate. The progression of these events is more or less predictable, which makes the analysis of these events useful to investigators seeking to account for the time that has passed since death, called the **post-mortem interval (PMI)**. The application of this knowledge—the profile of insect activity since death—to criminal investigation is called forensic entomology.

Flies will begin colonizing the orifices and any wounds present on the body of the recently deceased. Fly activity, especially egg-laying, sends a strong olfactory signal to other flies in the area so a body can quickly become swarmed. During this period of commotion, eggs are deposited continuously, producing young of varying ages present at the same time. The most important specimen collected by a forensic entomologist is the oldest life stage present on the body. This specimen acts as a stopwatch that began ticking the moment the first egg was deposited on the body. Using that species' life cycle timetable with local temperature and weather information, a forensic entomologist is able to approximate the PMI.

The life cycle of a blow fly begins with **oviposition**, or egg-laying. Development of the egg ends with an immature fly, called a larva or maggot, eclosing (hatching) from the egg. The larva molts (sheds its skin) three times during the larval phase. The individual between each of the molts is called an instar. Thus, there are three larval instars, each larger than the last. The larva will shed its skin three times, each time with a different set of appendages. Many species then proceed to the **migration** phase, wherein a larva stops feeding and travels several feet away from the corpse. The purpose of this travel is to allow the larva to pupate in a location some feet away from the environment which it used to call home. **Pupation** is marked by a hard shell the maggot secretes in which it will change from the larval to adult stage. The larval stage is protective in nature and some flies will remain as pupae for days

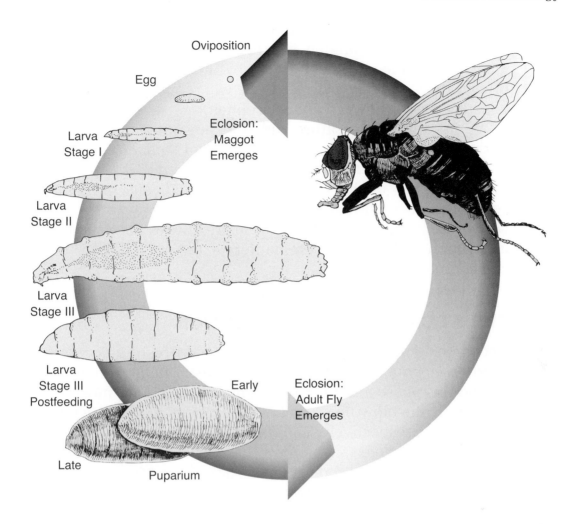

Oviposition

Egg

Larva
Stage I

Eclosion:
Maggot
Emerges

Larva
Stage II

Larva
Stage III

Larva
Stage III
Postfeeding

Early

Eclosion:
Adult Fly
Emerges

Late

Puparium

to weeks. After further development, an **adult** fly emerges from the pupa and begins the cycle anew. This describes the life cycle of the dozens of species we commonly refer to as "house flies." Blow flies and flesh flies are in this group, and these are the species to which we limit our exploration.

THE LIFE CYCLE

After eggs are laid, the duration of a typical blow fly life cycle is dependant on the temperature. It requires a certain time period, expressed as "degree-days" or "degree-hours," for the larva to develop. Degree days/hours are the number of days/hours multiplied by the number of degrees above a threshold temperature for that species (usually 50° Fahrenheit). This means that any time interval, say overnight, that is below 50° Fahrenheit does not count toward the life cycle—it is too cold for the eggs/larvae/puparia to grow. For example, at 70° Fahrenheit, eggs will hatch into larvae after approximately 12 hours. Larvae will pupate after approximately another 12 days, and adult flies will emerge from the puparia after approximately 8 more days. In other words, the complete life cycle will require 3 weeks at a constant temperature of 70° Fahrenheit.

Other than temperature, drugs or poisons in the decedent's bodily tissues can affect the growth rate of fly species. For example, arsenic, a heavy metal found in rat poison, slows down the growth rate of all fly species. More specifically, narcotics like cocaine can accelerate the growth rate, especially in the *Calliphora vomitoria* species. Factors like these are always important to the calculation of the post-mortem interval and must be carefully considered.

THE STAGES OF DECOMPOSITION

Decomposition of a mammal begins at the "fresh" stage and progresses until the body appears bloated. The flies that arrive during this phase are there within minutes, and are most commonly the blow flies and flesh flies, from genus *Calliphora* and *Sarcophaga*, respectively. The "bloated" stage occurs because of the activity of bacteria which produces gases inside the body. It is during this phase that house flies, from genus *Musca*, begin to appear and deposit eggs. The "decay" stage begins with the splitting of the skin to allow the gases to escape. The body then takes on a compressed appearance and exudes a powerful odor. By the end of this phase, the flesh is absent and only bone, skin, and hair remain. It is at this time that the larvae begin their migration away from the food source to find a suitable location to pupate. In the "post-decay" stage, beetles begin to colonize the body and consume the dry, less nutrient-rich components.

An important clue to the condition of a body at death is the location of the larval mass on a body. If an individual dies without sustaining a wound to the flesh—for example, by carbon monoxide asphyxiation—then the flies would initially lay their eggs in the orifices of the body. This grants the most convenient access through the tough skin. In this situation, the larvae are seen in the face/head and the anal/genital region first. If the larval mass is present in the chest or abdomen, this indicates there was an "unnatural orifice" in that area at the time of death. For example, if the decedent received a fatal stab wound to the abdomen, then a larval mass would be present in the trunk area, as well as the head and perineal regions.

EXERCISE 1 – ESTIMATING THE POST-MORTEM INTERVAL[18, 19]

In this exercise each team will be presented with "entomological evidence" collected from four death scenes. This "evidence" is simulated larvae and pupae, symbolized by pipe cleaners of varying colors and lengths. Teams use a ruler to measure the length of each "maggot." These data are then used in conjunction with Table 1 to identify the species present at the death scene and determine the post-mortem interval.

Color Key for Pipe Cleaners

White = *Sarcophaga*
Blue = *Musca*
Yellow = *Calliphora*
Pink = *Piophila*
Brown = pupa (species can only be determined by length of pupa)

Table 1 L=larva, E=egg, A=adult, P=pupa—Stage and Length in Millimeters for Each Species as Developed Under Constant 72° Fahrenheit.

SPECIES

Days after Death	Musca Domestica	Calliphora Vomitoria	Sarcophaga Carnaria	Piophila Nigirceps
1	~	E	L9–11	~
2	E	L9–11	L12–16	~
3	E	L9–11	L17–20	~
4	L6	L12–16	L21–25	~
5	L6	L12–16	L26–30	E
6	L7–11	L17–20	L31–35	E
7	L12–16	L17–20	L36–40	L3
8	L17–20	L21–25	L41–44	L3
9	L21–25	L21–25	L44–46	L4–6
10	L26–30	L26–30	L44–46	L7–9
11	L31–35	L26–30	P38–40	L10–13
12	P26–29	L31–35	P38–40	L14–16
13	P26–29	L31–35	P38–40	P13–15

(continued)

[18] Please refer to the *Instructor's Manual* for background information and instructions for the preparation of the materials used in this exercise.
[19] Adapted from "Of Maggots and Murder—Forensic Entomology in the Classroom" by Lisa Carloye, in *The American Biology Teacher, vol. 65*(5), May 2003.

Table 1 *Continued*

SPECIES

Days after Death	*Musca Domestica*	*Calliphora Vomitoria*	*Sarcophaga Carnaria*	*Piophila Nigirceps*
14	P26–29	P31–34	P38–40	P13–15
15	P26–29	P31–34	P38–40	P13–15
16	P26–29	P31–34	P38–40	P13–15
17	P26–29	P31–34	P38–40	P13–15
18	A30–32	P31–34	P38–40	P13–15
19		P31–34	A42–45	A16–18
20		P31–34		
21		A36–38		

Table 2 Factors Affecting the Development of Four Fly Species. Temperature Changes as from the Standard of 72° F, Given in Number of Days.

SPECIES

		Musca Domestica	*Calliphora Vomitoria*	*Sarcophaga Carnaria*	*Piophila Nigirceps*
Temperature (in°F)	55	Delayed 4	Delayed 4.5	Delayed 4	Delayed 3
	65	Delayed 2	Delayed 3	Delayed 2	Delayed 1
	80	Aaccelerated 1	Accelerated 2	Accelerated 1.5	Accelerated 1
	85	Accelerated 2	Accelerated 4	Accelerated 3	Accelerated 2
Environmental factors	Habitat	Urban/rural	Urban/rural	Urban/rural	Urban
	Lighting	Full to part sun	Part sun to shade	Prefers sun	Prefers sun
	Drugs	No effect	Sensitive to drugs	No effect	No effect

MATERIALS

Container of "maggots" and "puparia," supplied by your instructor
Ruler
Reference data and worksheet

PROCEDURE

1. Examine the "maggots" and "puparia" in your container. This represents the entomological evidence from a crime scene. Be careful to work with the evidence from one case at a time—do not mix up your cases!
2. Measure each "maggot" and record its length and color.

3. Compare these to the data provided in Table 1 to identify the species present in your "evidence" sample.

4. Based on the entomological evidence provided, you should make a conclusion about the earliest possible date of death in this case. Outline your findings in your notebook, citing specific examples from your analysis.

5. Answer the questions following each of the following cases. Document your findings (answers) in your notebook.

CASE A

Elderly male discovered in his home—apparently deceased for some time.

Maggots are apparent in his face and neck region.

Local temperature has been a consistent 70–75°F for the last 2 weeks.

Questions:

1. Approximately how long has this man been deceased?
2. Did you find maggots of different ages on the body?
3. Why or why not?

CASE B

Young male recovered in his college dorm room.

Maggots are evident in the man's head and chest regions.

The weather report shows daytime temperatures of 74–95°F with sunny skies.

The windows of his room are closed and the university keeps the building at a constant temperature of 72°F.

Questions:

1. Approximately how long has this man been deceased?
2. What effect, if any, does the outside temperature have on your estimation of the PMI?
3. How does the fact that the windows are closed influence your evidence sample?
4. How do you explain the absence of *Calliphora vomitoria*?
5. Do you suspect foul play? Explain.

CASE C

Adult female found in a city park.

The weather report indicates that the recent weather has been a heat wave with daytime temperatures at 84–86°F.

The toxicology report indicates the presence of cocaine in the woman's blood.

Questions:

1. Approximately how long has this woman been deceased?
2. What effect, if any, do the toxicological findings (cocaine in the woman's bodily fluids) have on your estimation of the PMI? Explain.
3. What effect, if any, does the daytime temperature have on your estimation of the PMI?
4. Do you suspect foul play? Why or why not?

CASE D

Adult male found by a road cleanup crew.

Maggots found in his face and neck region.

The subject was under tall trees on the side of an interstate highway in a rural area.

The weather has been partly sunny and 70–74°F for most of the week.

Questions:

1. Approximately how long has this man been deceased?
2. What effect, if any, does temperature have on your estimation of the PMI?
3. Does the death scene location, when compared to the entomological evidence, suggest foul play? Do you need more information to make this determination?

EXERCISE II – REARING MAGGOTS

In this exercise, you will observe the initial colonization activity of blow flies and subsequent larval development using a simulated corpse composed of fresh beef or chicken liver. Since fly activity is seasonal and temperature-dependent, it is necessary to perform this lab during a warm week, with a daytime temperature of *at least* 65°F (18°C).

SAFETY

MATERIALS

One (1) three-pound coffee can, with lid

One hole paper punch

¼ lb. fresh beef or chicken liver

5-inch square of aluminum foil

Vermiculite

Timer

Outdoor thermometer

Specimen jars

Marker

Isopropyl alcohol

Magnifying hand lens

A reference collection is a set of life stages from one or more species of flies kept for the purposes of comparison to recovered specimens. Your instructor will find a useful reference collection kit—*Maggots from Murder,* available at http://www.maggotsfrommurder.com, to help you determine the growth stage of the maggots you recovered.

PROCEDURE

1. In the lab, remove the lid from your coffee can and make ten or fifteen holes with the one-hole paper punch. These holes will provide access to the food source for the adult flies.

2. Add approximately ½ inch of vermiculite to the bottom of the can.

3. Fashion a tray of aluminum foil around the liver. This will help to contain the liver during larval development.

4. Put the liver in the can and affix the lid.

5. Select a shady spot outdoors and away from any heat sources for your simulated death scene.

6. Note the time and date when you place the can on the ground.

7. Retrieve the can after 24 hours.

8. Using your magnifying lens, remove a few eggs from the surface of the "body" and transfer them to a specimen jar containing isopropyl alcohol. Label the jar with the contents, date, time, and your initials.

9. Sketch the eggs in your notebook.

10. Place the can in a well-ventilated area in your laboratory and observe the progress of the larvae over the next 3 weeks. Record the temperature of the room every day.

Plan Your Experiment

Plan the following observations:

1. Appearance of larvae
2. Appearance of migrating larvae
3. Formation of puparia
4. Appearance of adult flies

The room temperature will determine the time of these events relative to the time of oviposition. *It is up to you to estimate when each of these phases will occur.*

Make Your Observations

1. For each of the phases previously described (from egg to adult), remove a specimen of the appropriate life stage and rinse with water to remove as much of the substrate as possible.
2. Transfer to a specimen jar containing isopropyl alcohol.
3. Label the jar with the contents, date, time, and your initials.
4. Using your stereoscopic microscope, examine the specimen and sketch it in the best detail you can.
5. Measure the approximate dimensions of each specimen and include this information in your report.

Forensic Anthropology[20]

CASE HISTORY

John Wayne Gacy

On a cold December day in 1978, police entered the home of John Wayne Gacy, Jr., a known sexual offender. They were there to investigate the disappearance of a 15-year-old boy who had been offered a job by Gacy. A search of the Gacy house ultimately revealed a number of incriminating items related to the disappearances of other youngsters. Gacy finally confessed to police that he killed at least thirty people and buried most of the remains of the victims under the crawl space of his house. Buried beneath the crawl space or in his garage were twenty-eight young male victims. Gacy disposed of five bodies in a nearby river when he ran out of room in the crawl space, and because he had been experiencing back problems digging the graves. Police faced the horrific responsibility of identifying the remains of the victims.

The victims were so alike in age, race, and stature that police initially were unable to make individual identifications for most of the victims. Some of the victims had been buried on top of older graves, co-mingling their remains. Clyde Snow, the world-renowned forensic anthropologist from Oklahoma, was asked to help investigators make the difficult identifications.

Snow began by examining each skeleton to make sure each of the bones was correctly attributed to an individual. Once he was sure all the bones were sorted properly, the in-depth study began. Long bones like the femur (thigh bone) were used to estimate each individual's height. This helped to narrow the search when attempting to match the victims with

---

[20] Please refer to the *Instructor's Manual* for additional preparation instructions relating to this experiment.

the descriptions of missing persons. Next, Snow made a thirty-five-point examination of each skull for comparison to known individuals.

After narrowing the possibilities to those missing persons fitting the general description, investigators were left with their hospital and dental records. Evidence of injury, illness, surgery, or other unique skeletal defects were used to make an identification. Snow also pointed out features which gave clues to the victims' behavior and medical history. He discovered that one of Gacy's victims had an old fracture of his left arm, and that his left scapula (shoulder blade) and arm bore the tell-tale signs of a left-handed individual. These details were matched to a missing persons' report and another young victim was identified.

For the most difficult cases, Snow called in the help of forensic sculptor and facial reconstructionist Betty Pat Gatliff. She used clay and depth markers to put the flesh back on the faces of these forgotten boys in the hopes that someone would recognize them after their photographs were released to the media. While her reconstruction efforts were successful, not a single definite identification resulted. Investigators found some families unwilling to accept the idea that their loved one was one of Gacy's victims. Even with Gatliff's help, nine of Gacy's victims remain unidentified.

In 1994, Gacy was executed by lethal injection.

THE MISSION OF THE FORENSIC ANTHROPOLOGIST

The function of a forensic anthropologist entails four essential components relative to assisting criminal investigation:

1. To investigate and interpret the crime scene and/or burial site, called **taphonomy**;
2. To develop a **biological profile** of the recovered remains;
3. To report and interpret any **evidence of trauma** or injury apparent on the bones; and
4. To determine the **identity** of the recovered individual.

An anthropologist is called into an investigation when skeletal remains are discovered. This usually means that the crime scene is old, and the decedent has been missing for a long time. This presents particular difficulties for police. The chances of quickly identifying the decedent are slim. Here is a common scenario: the decedent cannot be identified from a photograph in a missing persons' file, he or she most likely is not carrying identification, and any casual relationships, employment history, or last-known sightings are long forgotten by the community. The passage of time, which can be months or even years, makes a crime much more difficult to solve.

Significant knowledge of human anatomy and physiology must be brought to bear on the questions posited by an old crime scene, and an anthropologist must pay particular attention to the context in which the evidence is found. The surrounding landscape, soil, and even the position of the remains can be just as important as the bones themselves to solving a case.

ANATOMICAL TERMS

Some common terms used in the description and analysis of skeletal remains appear in the following list. It is important to note that these terms are used to describe a location, such as an injury found on a bone, *relative to* another anatomical landmark or location. For example, one would not describe a person's wrist as merely *distal*. Examples of proper usage are listed after each term. To the right of these, list an example of your own.

Anterior—in front of
- *The heart is anterior to the spine.*

Posterior—in back of
- *The throat is posterior to the teeth.*

Superior—above, closer to the head-end
- *The shoulders are superior to the hips.*

Inferior—below, closer to the foot-end
- *The tongue is inferior to the palate.*

Lateral—closer to the side of, farther away from the midline
- *The ribs are lateral to the sternum.*

Medial—farther from the side of, closer to the midline
- *The nose is medial to the eyes.*

Proximal—closer to the center of the body
- *The elbow is proximal to the wrist.*

Distal—farther from the center of the body
- *The ankle is distal to the knee.*

EXERCISE 1

COMPARATIVE ANATOMY

The single most important determination an anthropologist makes about skeletal remains is the species. Before a murder investigation can begin, a human death must be proved. For this reason, forensic anthropologists must be familiar with both human and animal skeletal morphology.

Visit http://www.eskeletons.org to practice comparing skulls and jaws of primates. Select the "comparative anatomy" page and choose the "skeletal element" and "species" you want to observe. Select "human" and then "side by side comparison." Then choose the gorilla. This will present you with the photos of a human skull and a gorilla skull on the same page for direct comparison. Use your left mouse button to click on a bone. The name of each bone will appear in the drop-down menu to the left. Alternately, you can select a bone by name and it will be highlighted on both skulls.

SPECIES COMPARISON

Notice the difference between the canine teeth in the gorilla and in the human jaw. The gorilla's canines are enormous compared to the human. What do you think this says about the function each species' teeth must perform? The gorilla spends most of its day chewing on dense vegetation and using its large teeth as tools. Humans perform the same function by using intellect to make tools, resulting in a reduced need for large, pointy teeth and a strong jaw.

Next, notice how much larger the human braincase is than the gorilla's. This is a direct result of our larger brain, the organ that makes humans unique. Change the view from frontal to lateral, and then to caudal. Practice manipulating the view of the skull. Find the jaw bone in each view and use it as a point of reference.

Now, what can you determine by comparing the human and chimpanzee skulls? And the chimpanzee and gorilla?

EXERCISE 2

DETERMINATION OF SEX

The skeletal remains that a forensic anthropologist receives are often without known identity. The most important factor to this determination is the portion of the skeleton that is recovered. The most informative portions of the human skeleton relative to the determination of sex are the skull, the pelvis, the femur, and the humerus.

Sexual dimorphism, the difference in size or shape between males and females of a species, is present in many of the animals you see every day. The best examples are found in birds, whose size and plumage can vary dramatically between the male and female (e.g., a rooster and a chicken). This exists in humans as well, but not to such an extreme.

Although male students may be on average taller than female students, this is not always true. Each skeleton must be examined at various locations to determine its sex, but correct determination is not guaranteed. Even when an expert uses the cranium, the most reliable skeletal element for this determination, he or she is correct only 80–90 percent of the time.[21] In addition, these differences are found most prominently in adults. Sex determination in children is much more difficult.

These anatomical differences that differentiate a male from a female are outlined at http://medstat.med.utah.edu/kw/osteo/forensics.

Choose the link to "Forensic Anthropology." Next, select "Age, Sex, and Stature." Next, choose "Determining Sex," and finally, "From the Skull." This side-by-side comparison of male and female skulls clearly shows the larger size of the male skull and canine teeth, as well as the differences in the shape of the jaw bone (mandible), or brow bone (frontal bone).

The male skeleton is, in general, larger or more **robust** than the female. The term used to describe a less robust skeleton is **gracile**. This is the most general factor used for sex determination. The shape of the bony features of the skull is different between men and women due to the reduced muscle mass present in the average female skull.

Next, select "From the Pelvis" and explore the fundamental differences present between male and female pelves. The most dramatic differences are in the greater sciatic notch, the subpubic angle. In addition, the male and female pelvis are functionally different because the female pelvis is required to accommodate pregnancy and childbirth.

After that, select "From the Femur" and be sure to note the size differences between male and female thigh bones. Also obvious from this comparison is that the male joints are larger than those of the female. Change the view from anterior to lateral and then to inferior. Notice how the typical female femur is more gracile at every angle. Note: The femurs pictured are for the purposes of demonstrating sexual dimorphism present in the human species. There is natural variation between individuals which makes these statements true only *most of the time*.

---

[21] White, T. D. *Human Osteology,* 2nd edition (New York: Academic Press, 2000).

EXERCISE 3

EMPIRICAL MEASUREMENT OF SEX DIFFERENCES[22]

When you meet someone for the first time, your brain automatically recognizes dozens of attributes that aid in your most basic assessment of the individual. Young or old? Healthy or ill? Male or female? The visual cues your brain uses to ascribe a gender to a face are subtle and difficult to target. As previously mentioned, the condition that men and women look different is called sexual dimorphism, and millions of species use this to identify potential mates, potential rivals, and even potential predators. These differences develop during puberty and are not clearly identifiable until sexual maturity. For this reason, children and adolescents do not provide reliable results for this kind of determination.

Sexual dimorphism can be identified in the human skeleton by measuring the bones of males and females, compiling these data, and determining the average measurement for each sex. If the average measurements are different, you have proved a dimorphic condition. You can apply these findings in later investigations to determine the sex of an unknown individual. There are numerous locations that can be used to make this determination, but you will focus on the skull and hand in this exercise.

PART I

Use a ruler to measure the height (chin to scalp) and width (ear lobe to ear lobe) of six adult men and six adult women. Record these data below:

Chin to Scalp

Men	Women
_____	_____
_____	_____
_____	_____
_____	_____
_____	_____
_____	_____

Calculate the Average

_____   _____

[22] Courtesy of Thomas Crist, PhD, State University of New York, Utica, N.Y.

Ear Lobe to Ear Lobe

Men		Women
_____		_____
_____		_____
_____		_____
_____		_____
_____		_____
_____	**Calculate the** **Average**	_____

PART II

Use a ruler to measure the distance across the knuckles of the hand at the base of the index finger to the base of the little finger. Record your results for six adult men and six adult women below:

Men		Women
_____		_____
_____		_____
_____		_____
_____		_____
_____		_____
_____	**Calculate the** **Average**	_____

EXERCISE 4

HUMAN DENTITION

Your teeth are unique. The size, pattern, and orientation of your teeth, taken together, create a unique profile that can be seen when you bite down on a malleable object. Forensic odontologists can use this feature to match bite marks found on an object or skin to a suspect.

1. Divide the class into groups with three students each.
2. Use scissors to remove the bottom of a Styrofoam cup.
3. Next, cut the cup into thirds from the lip to the base. You should be left with three strips, one for each student in the group. Each strip should have the approximate dimensions of 3 inches wide by the original height of the cup.
4. Flatten your piece of Styrofoam by gently bending it. It does not have to be perfectly flat. Label a corner of the Styrofoam with your initials *on both sides.*
5. Gently bite down on the Styrofoam so that your incisors and canine teeth are in contact with the material. DO NOT BITE THROUGH IT!
6. Carefully wipe any saliva away with a tissue. Label each side with "UPPER" and "LOWER."
7. Take your Styrofoam dental impression to a copy machine and copy each side. Be sure your initials are visible.
8. Compare your images to those of your classmates. Are any identical?
9. Measure the distance between the canine teeth of your upper and lower jaw. Compile these measurements from your class into two groups, male and female. Find the average of these measurements. Is there a difference? Why or why not? (Hint: Consider the ages of the students in your class. What would you expect from a group of adolescents versus adults?)

EXERCISE 5

BITE MARK CASES

You are investigating an assault involving bite mark evidence. The bite patterns taken from two suspects, A and B, and bite mark evidence from the victim follow. Compare each suspect's dentition to the wound pattern present on the victim and see if you can make a determination as to either suspect's involvement in the crime. Teachers should consult Chapter 3 of the *Instructor's Manual.*

Case 1[23]   Bite Mark from Victim

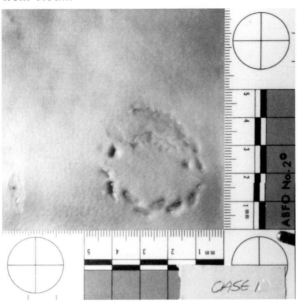

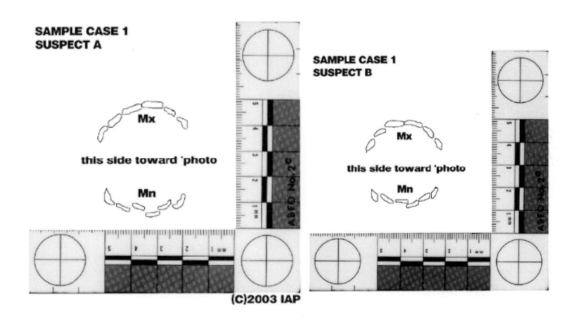

---

[23] Case photographs courtesy of Dr. Iain A. Pretty, University of Manchester, U.K., School of Dentistry.

Case 2 Bite Mark from Victim

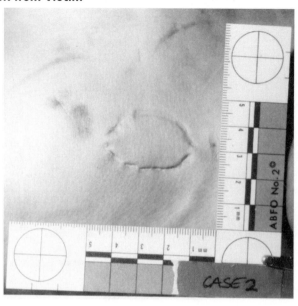

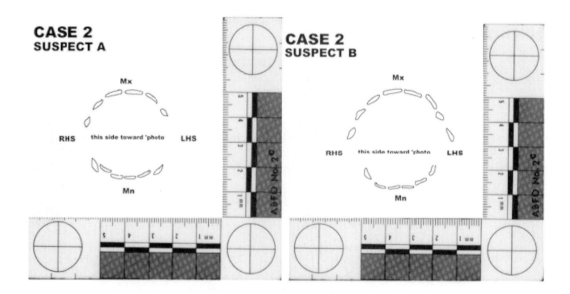

Case 3   Bite Mark from Victim

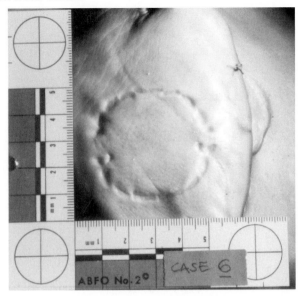

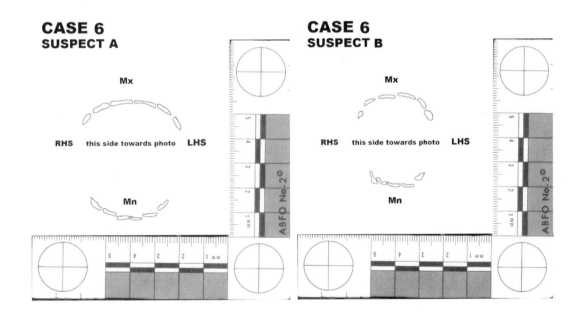

CASE 6
SUSPECT A

Mx

RHS   this side towards photo   LHS

Mn

CASE 6
SUSPECT B

Mx

RHS   this side towards photo   LHS

Mn